ESSENT

GW01019500

COSTA BRAVA

Original text by Tony Kelly
Updated by Tony Kelly

© Automobile Association Developments Limited 2008
First published 2008

ISBN 978-0-7495-5354-8

Published by AA Publishing, a trading name of Automobile Association Developments Limited, whose registered office is Fanum House, Basing View, Basingstoke, Hampshire RG21 4EA.
Registered number 1878835.

Colour separation: MRM Graphics Ltd
Printed and bound in Italy by Printer Trento S.r.l.

A03164
Maps in this title produced by Global Mapping, Brackley, UK. Licence no – 07/021.
Copyright © Global Mapping/Cartografia 2007

About this book

This book is divided into five sections.

The essence of the Costa Brava
pages 6–19
Introduction; Features; Food and Drink;
Short Break including the 10 Essentials

Planning pages 20–33
Before You Go; Getting There; Getting
Around; Being There

Best places to see pages 34–55
The unmissable highlights of any visit
to the Costa Brava

Best things to do pages 56–77
Good places to have lunch; places to
take the children; best beaches; best
golf courses and more

Exploring pages 78–185
The best places to visit in the Costa
Brava, organized by area

Maps
All map references are to the maps on
the covers. For example, Castellfollit de
la Roca has the reference ✚ 4D –
indicating the grid square in which it is
to be found

Admission prices
Inexpensive (under €3.50)
Moderate (€3.50–€10)
Expensive (over €10)

Hotel prices
Prices are for a double room per night in
summer including breakfast and 7 per
cent VAT: € budget (under €75); €€
moderate (€75–€150); €€€ (over €150)

Restaurant prices
Prices are for a three-course meal per
person without drinks and service:
€ budget (under €20); €€ moderate
(€20–€40); €€€ (over €40)

Contents

BEST THINGS TO DO

56 – 77

EXPLORING...

78 – 185

The essence of...

You cannot separate the Costa Brava from Catalonia.
History has given the Cataláns a fiercely independent
spirit, looking outwards, to Europe, as much as in,
to the Iberian peninsula. The first Greek and Roman
settlers landed here; French art and architecture
crossed into Spain over the Pyrenees. It is no surprise
that this is where Spain's large-scale tourist industry
began. The Cataláns are courteous, businesslike,
conservative and welcoming, but with little of the
flamboyance of their Spanish neighbours. In the
Mediterranean way, they know how to take life
slowly – but also how to get things done.

THE ESSENCE OF COSTA BRAVA

features

Costa Brava – 'the Wild Coast'.
The name was coined by a local
journalist, Ferran Agulló, in
1908, gazing out at the rugged
coastline of pine-clad cliffs and
coves. At times you could be
forgiven for thinking he was
referring to the nightlife, rather
than the scenery.

GEOGRAPHY AND CLIMATE

- The Costa Brava begins at Blanes, 60km (37 miles) north of Barcelona, and continues around the coast for 220km (137 miles) to the French border at Portbou.
- There are 119 official beaches, with a total length of 56km (35 miles) – a quarter of the entire coastline.

● The average summer temperature is 26°C (79°F), and there are more than 200 days of sunshine a year. The sea temperature reaches 24°C (75°F) in August and is pleasantly warm from June to October. The *tramuntana*, a cold north wind, can strike at any time.

GOVERNMENT AND ECONOMY

● The Costa Brava belongs to Girona province, itself part of Catalunya (Catalonia), a semi-autonomous region of Spain since 1979. Catalonia is the wealthiest region in Spain, producing 20 per cent of the country's gross national product.

PEOPLE

● The population of the Costa Brava region rises from around 425,000 in winter to a million in summer. The capital, Girona, has a population of 75,000. Catalonia has the highest population density of any region in Spain.

TOURISM

● More than five million foreign tourists visit the Costa Brava each year. The majority are from France, Germany and the UK. There is also a growing number of foreigners owning second homes in the region.

● The Costa Brava is the favourite holiday destination among Cataláns, who make two million visits to the area each year.

● In the peak of the tourist season the Costa Brava can offer visitors more than 80,000 hotel beds, 100,000 pitches in campsites and 500,000 places in self-catering villas and apartments.

food & drink

Catalán cooking is one of the great cuisines of Europe, with the produce of the sea and the mountains enhanced by many foreign influences. The Romans introduced olives and planted vines; the Arabs brought saffron, almonds and dried fruit. The essential flavours are Mediterranean – olive oil, garlic, onions, tomatoes, peppers – and the latest trend towards 'modern Catalán' cuisine combines traditional ingredients with French and Italian styles.

MAIN MEALS

The most characteristic style of cooking is known as *mar i muntanya* (mountain and sea). This

produces unusual combinations, like chicken with lobster, rabbit with snails and pigs' trotters stuffed with prawns. Paella comes into this category too – a mound of steaming saffron rice which might be topped with just about any combination of meat, seafood and snails.

Meat is always excellent, especially veal from Girona and lamb from Ripoll. Duck might be accompanied by either turnips or pears. One famous meat dish is *escudella i carn d'olla*, a hearty boiled meat casserole which is traditionally served at Christmas; the broth is eaten with pasta shells as a starter, with the meat to follow. The Cataláns are particularly proud of their many pork sausages: popular varieties include *botifarra, bisbe, llonganissa* and *fuet*. Some are eaten raw, like a salami, but *botifarra* is usually grilled and served with white beans.

Fish and seafood are served all along the coast, often simply grilled with a *romesco* (tomato, almond and pepper) sauce. Hake, monkfish and sole are widely

available; sea-bass and mullet are more expensive. *Suquet de peix* is a delicious casserole of white fish and potatoes, poached in white wine.

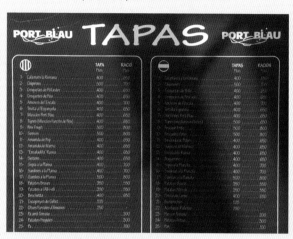

SNACKS, SALADS AND STARTERS

Tapas bars serve a bewildering range of snacks, from meatballs to octopus, in saucer-size portions. The classic bar snack is a plate of *pa amb tomàquet* – bread rubbed with tomato, drizzled with olive oil and topped with thin slices of cheese or cured mountain ham. Most bars keep a selection of *truitas* – cold potato omelettes, sometimes flavoured with spinach, artichoke or courgette. A Catalán salad *(amanida)* makes a meal in itself – piles of lettuce, tomato, olives and onions with a selection of cold meats, cheeses, tuna and egg. Other popular starters include *escalivada* (grilled

pepper and aubergine salad) and *esqueixada*, a salad topped with shredded salt cod.

DESSERTS

Spain is not known for its desserts but Catalonia produces two of the best – *crema catalána*, an egg custard with a caramelized sugar crust, and *mel i mató*, curd cheese with honey. In most eating places you are likely to be offered a choice between fresh fruit, ice-cream and *flan* (caramel custard).

short break

If you only have a short time to visit the Costa Brava and would like to take home some unforgettable memories, you can do something local and capture the real flavour of the area. The following suggestions will give you a wide range of sights and experiences that won't take long, won't cost very much and will make your visit very special.

● **Follow the winding coast road** from Tossa de Mar to Sant Feliu (➤ 164–165), then explore the rocky coves around Begur and Palafrugell that gave the Costa Brava its name.

● **Go diving or snorkelling** in the waters around the Medes islands (➤ 100), where the reefs and caves harbour an abundance of underwater life.

● **Visit the fish markets** in Blanes, Palamós and Roses, then dine out-of-doors on some of the freshest seafood you will ever eat.

● **Relax in the botanical gardens** at Cap Roig and Blanes (➤ 97, 159), where Mediterranean plants grow on cliffsides overlooking the sea.

● **Wander the back streets of Girona**, with its carefully restored Jewish quarter and medieval mansions (➤ 82–92).

- **Visit the surreal Dalí museum** in Figueres (➤ 52–53), then follow the Salvador Dalí trail from Portlligat to Puból (➤ 144–145).

- **Head for one of the inland towns on market day** for a real taste of Catalán life. One of the best is the Saturday market at Vic (➤ 172).

- **Browse in the pottery shops** of La Bisbal (➤ 95) and take home a souvenir of your visit.

● **Take a boat trip** along the coast around the wild northern coastline between Roses and Cap de Creus.

● **Lie on the beach** soaking up the sun – the authentic Costa Brava experience. But don't forget your sunblock!

Planning

Before you go

WHEN TO GO

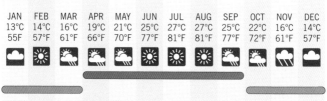

JAN	FEB	MAR	APR	MAY	JUN	JUL	AUG	SEP	OCT	NOV	DEC
13°C	14°C	16°C	19°C	21°C	25°C	27°C	27°C	25°C	22°C	16°C	14°C
55F	57°F	61°F	66°F	70°F	77°F	81°F	81°F	77°F	72°F	61°F	57°F

🔴 High season 🔵 Low season

The above temperatures are the average daily maximum for each month on the coast. Sunshine is almost guaranteed throughout the summer, particularly during the peak tourist season of July and August. If you want to avoid the crowds but still enjoy warm, sunny weather, the best months to visit are May, June and September. These are also the best times for activities such as walking, cycling and golf. Between October and April, many hotels close their doors and resorts which are lively in summer have a distinct off-season feel.

Girona is busy throughout the year. Away from the coast, the weather is more unpredictable. You should always take warm clothes and be prepared for wind, rain and snow in mountain areas.

WHAT YOU NEED

- ● Required
- ○ Suggested
- ▲ Not required

Contact your travel agent or the U.S. embassy for the current regulations regarding passports and visas. Your passport should be valid for at least six months beyond date of entry.

	UK	Germany	USA	Netherlands
Passport/National Identity Card	●	●	●	●
Visa (Regulations can change – check before you travel)	▲	▲	●	▲
Onward or Return Ticket	▲	▲	●	▲
Health Inoculations	▲	▲	▲	▲
Health Documentation (▶ 23, Health Advice)	●	●	●	●
Travel Insurance	○	○	●	○
Driving Licence (National)	●	●	●	●
Car Insurance Certificate	●	●	●	●

WEBSITES
www.costabrava.org

www.catalunyatourism.com

TOURIST OFFICES AT HOME
In the UK
Spanish Tourist Office
PO Box 4009, London W1A 6NB
☎ 020 7486 8077;
www.tourspain.co.uk

In the USA
Tourist Office of Spain
666 Fifth Avenue (35th Floor)

New York, NY 10103
☎ 212/265-8822

Tourist Office of Spain
8383 Wilshire Boulevard
Suite 960, Beverly Hills
CA 90211
☎ 323/658-7192
www.spain.info

HEALTH INSURANCE
Citizens of European Union countries are entitled to free reciprocal health care in Spain on production of anEHIC (European Health Insurance Card). Private medical insurance is still advisable for emergencies, and is essential for all non-European Union visitors.

ADVANCE PASSENGER INFORMATION (API)
Passengers on all flights to and from Spain now have to supply advance passenger information to the Spanish authorities – full given names, surname, nationality, date of birth and travel document details, namely a passport number. Some airports may have a self-service kiosk for this, otherwise staff at check-in desks will be able to collect the information.

TIME DIFFERENCES

GMT	Costa Brava	Germany	USA (NY)	Netherlands	Spain
12 noon	1PM	1PM	7AM	1PM	1PM

Like the rest of Spain, Catalonia is one hour ahead of Greenwich Mean Time (GMT+1), except from late March to late October, when summer time (GMT+2) operates.

NATIONAL HOLIDAYS

1 Jan *New Year's Day*
6 Jan *Epiphany*
Mar/Apr *Good Friday,*
Easter Monday
1 May *Labour Day*
24 Jun *St John's Day*
15 Aug *Assumption of the*
Virgin

11 Sep *Catalan National*
Day
12 Oct *Spanish National*
Day
1 Nov *All Saints' Day*
6 Dec *Constitution Day*
8 Dec *Feast of the*
Immaculate Conception

25 Dec *Christmas Day*
26 Dec *St Stephen's Day*
Most shops, banks and
offices close on these days
but many places stay open
in the main resorts.
Museums observe Sunday
opening times.

WHAT'S ON WHEN

January *Els Tres Reis* (5–6 Jan): children across Catalonia receive their
Christmas presents when the Three Kings arrive in towns and villages by
boat or on horseback.
February *Carnestoltes*: pre-Lenten carnival parades (see panel).
March/April *Setmana Santa* (Holy Week): on the evening of Maundy
Thursday, men and boys dressed as skeletons march through Verges, near
Torroella de Montgrí, performing a medieval 'dance of death'. Girona's
Good Friday procession re-enacts Christ's death, with his crucified body
carried to the cathedral by actors dressed as Roman soldiers. There is also

a crucifixion ceremony on Good Friday in Sant Hilari Sacalm.

Festa de Sant Jordi (23 Apr): book and flower markets are set up in the streets in honour of Catalonia's patron, St George. The biggest festivities take place along the Rambla in Girona.

May *Carroussel Costa Brava* (Whit Sunday): Palafrugell's Spring Festival was begun in 1963 to continue the carnival traditions following its prohibition. The highlight is the parade of floats on the Sunday afternoon.

June *Festa de Sant Joan* (23–24 Jun): the eve of the feast of St John is marked with bonfires and firework parties all over Catalonia.

July *Cantada d'Havaneres* (1st Sat): traditional sea-shanties on the beach at Calella de Palafrugell.

Aplec de la Sardana (2nd Sun): the biggest *sardana* festival takes place in Olot.

Mare de Déu del Carme (16 Jul): processions of fishing boats in the main ports in honour of the protector of fishermen.

Festa de Santa Cristina (24–26 Jul): Moorish dancing and a mass pilgrimage by boat from Lloret de Mar to the hermitage of Santa Cristina.

August *Cantada d'Havaneres* (1st Sat): traditional sea shanties on the beach at Llafranc.

Mayor's Sardana (16 Aug): open spiral dance held at night in Amer, west of Girona.

September *Festa del Tura* (8 Sep): processions of giants, dwarves and hobby-horses in the streets of Olot.

La Diada (11 Sep): Catalonia's national day is marked all over the region by fireworks, street parades and *sardana* dancing.

October *Festa de Sant Narcís* (late Oct): a fortnight of festivities in Girona, featuring bullfights, bonfires and parades of giants.

December *Nadal* (Christmas, 24–25 Dec): midnight Mass is celebrated in churches across the region.

Carnival The pre-Lenten carnival, with its riotous street parades and fancy dress balls, was banned under the Franco dictatorship, but has returned with a vengeance. Every town on the Costa Brava seems to organize its own Carnival festivities, and the processions of floats at Platja d'Aro and Palamós, on the weekend before Shrove Tuesday, are some of the biggest in Spain. Carnival ends with the 'burial of the sardine', signifying the end of winter.

Getting there

BY AIR

Barcelona (El Prat) Airport

100km (62 miles) to Girona

2 hours

N/A

90 minutes

Girona-Costa Brava Airport

11km (7 miles) to Girona

N/A

30 minutes

20 minutes

Girona-Costa Brava airport (☎ 972 18 66 00) is served by regular flights from London, Paris, Rome and other European cities. There are several flights a day from the UK by Ryanair (☎ 807 22 02 20; www.ryanair.com) as well as additional charter flights in summer. Barcelona Bus (☎ 902 36 15 50) operates shuttle buses from the airport into central Girona and also to the main resorts. A wider range of scheduled carriers, including the Spanish national airline Iberia, fly into Barcelona airport.

BY CAR
European route E15 connects Paris to Barcelona and travels through the Costa Brava region. From Paris, it follows the A6 motorway to Lyon, then the A7 to Orange and A9 to Perpignan, before crossing the border at La Jonquera where it becomes the Spanish AP7. It is best to allow two days for the journey. Alternatively, take a car ferry from the UK to Northern Spain and join the Spanish motorway network from Bilbao to Barcelona.

BY TRAIN
Girona and Figueres are both stops on the high-speed rail link from Paris to Barcelona, which crosses into Spain at Portbou. The Elipsos train network links Paris, Zurich and Milan with Girona and Barcelona, using comfortable overnight 'train hotels'. For UK bookings, contact Rail Europe (0870 837 1371; www.raileurope.co.uk).

Getting around

PUBLIC TRANSPORT

Trains The main line from Barcelona to France passes through the Costa Brava region, with regular stops at Girona, Figueres and Portbou. There is also a branch line linking Barcelona and Girona with Blanes. For information on train services, call RENFE on ☎ 902 24 02 02; www.renfe.es

Buses A wide network of local bus routes, operated by a number of private companies, the largest being Sarfa, connects Girona and Figueres with the main towns and villages of the Costa Brava. Extra routes connect the coastal resorts in summer. Timetables change, so check with your local tourist office or at the nearest bus station.

Boats A regular boat service connects the resorts of Blanes, Lloret de Mar and Tossa de Mar between April and October, with some boats continuing north as far as Palamós. There are departures at least hourly, calling at various beaches along the way, so you can use this service for day-trips to nearby beaches and coves. There are also a number of cruises in summer from all the major resorts, including Cadaqués, Roses, Empúria-brava, L'Estartit and Sant Feliu de Guíxols – details can be found on the quayside at noticeboards and ticket kiosks. One popular trip is the cruise to the Illes Medes (Medes Islands) on a glass-hulled boat from L'Estartit (➤ 99).

FARES AND TICKETS

Students/Youths Holders of an International Student Identity Card (ISIC) may be able to obtain some concessions on travel and entrance fees. Anyone under 26 or belonging to a national youth hostel organisation can stay cheaply at the hostels *(albergues de joventut)* in Girona, Banyoles, Olot and Empúries.

Senior citizens There are few specific discounts available for senior citizens, though it is always worth checking at museums and tourist attractions. A number of hotels and tour operators offer economical deals on long-stay winter holidays, when the savings in the cost of fuel bills can almost wipe out the cost of the trip.

TAXIS

Taxis can be hired at ranks or by flagging down a taxi with a green light on the roof. Prices are good, but there are supplements for late night, weekend and public holiday travel as well as for luggage and long-distance journeys, so check in advance.

DRIVING

- The Spanish drive on the right side of the road.

- Seat belts must be worn at all times. Children under 12 must use an approved child seat/harness

- Random breath-testing is carried out. Never drive under the influence of alcohol.

- Fuel *(gasolina)* is sold in various grades, including unleaded *(sense plomb)* and super-unleaded and diesel *(gasoil)*. A few petrol stations are self-service but most have an attendant. Credit cards are widely accepted and at some you can pay at the pump using your card.

- Speed limits are as follows:
  Motorways (autopistas – toll payable): 120kph (74mph)
  Main roads: 100kph (62mph)
  Minor roads 90kph/56mph)
  Urban roads: 50kph (31mph)

- If you are driving your own car in Spain it is a good idea to take out European breakdown cover before you leave. Members of AIT-affiliated motoring clubs, including the AA, can use the services of the Real Automóvil Club de España (RACE ☎ 902 40 45 45). Car-rental firms provide their own rescue service.

CAR RENTAL

The leading international car rental companies have offices at Barcelona and Girona airports. There are local companies in the resorts. Keep hire documents, your driving licence and your passport with you at all times.

Being there

TOURIST OFFICES

Blanes
Passeig de Catalunya 2
☎ 972 33 03 48

Figueres
Plaça del Sol
☎ 972 50 31 55

Girona
Rambla de la Llibertat 1
☎ 972 22 65 75

Lloret de Mar
Passeig Camprodón i Arrieta 1
☎ 972 36 47 35

Olot
Carrer del'Hospici 8
☎ 972 26 01 41

Palafrugell
Plaça del'Església
☎ 972 30 02 28

Tossa de Mar
Avinguda del Pelegrí 25
☎ 972 34 01 08

Vic
Carrer Ciutat 4
☎ 938 86 20 91

The above offices are open throughout the year. Most towns and villages have offices open in summer; look out for the international L sign.

The staff are usually multilingual and helpful and can supply you with local maps and guides.

Information about the Costa Brava can also be found at www.costabrava.org

MONEY

The euro (€) is the official currency of Spain, divided into 100 cents (or *centesimi*). Coins come in denominations of 1, 2, 5, 10, 20 and 50 cents, 1 and 2 euros, and bank notes come in denominations of 5, 10, 20, 50, 100, 200 and 500 euros (the last two are rarely seen). The notes and one side of the coins are the same throughout the European single currency zone, but each country has a different design on one face of each of the coins. Bank notes and coins from any of the other countries can be used in Spain.

TIPS/GRATUITIES

Yes ✓   No ✗

Restaurants	✓ 10%
Cafés/bars	✓ change
Taxis	✓ 10%
Tour guides (discretionary)	✓ €1–2
Chambermaids/porters	✓ €1–2
Toilet attendants	✗

POSTAL SERVICES

Post offices *(Correus)* are generally open Monday–Saturday 9am–1pm. Stamps *(segells)* can also be bought at kiosks and at *estancs* (tobacconists' shops).

TELEPHONES

Public telephones take euro coins as well as phonecards *(teletarjetas)*, which can be bought at post offices or tobacconists. Most also accept credit cards. The cheap rate for international calls is weekdays 10pm–8am, after 2pm Saturday and all day Sunday.

International dialling codes

From Spain to
UK: 00 44
Germany: 00 49

USA & Canada: 00 1
Netherlands: 00 31

Emergency telephone numbers

Police (Policía Nacional/Mosso d'Esquadra): 112
Fire (Bombers): 112

Ambulance (Ambulància): 112
In any emergency you can ring 112

EMBASSIES AND CONSULATES

UK: ☎ 93 366 6200
Germany: ☎ 93 292 10 00

USA: ☎ 93 280 2227
Netherlands: ☎ 93 410 62 10

HEALTH ADVICE

Sun advice Avoid the midday sun and use a high-factor sun block. Children are particularly vulnerable and should always wear a hat.

Drugs Prescription and non-prescription drugs are available from pharmacies *(farmàcies)*, distinguished by a large green cross. Recreational drugs, which you may be offered at nightclubs in the larger resorts, are illegal and should be avoided.

Safe water Tap water is generally safe to drink, but mineral water is cheap and easy to buy, either sparkling *(amb gas)* or still *(sense gas)*.

PERSONAL SAFETY

In an emergency, ask for the nearest police station *(comissaria)* and speak to the Policía Nacional, known in Catalonia as the Mossos d'Esquadra. Take sensible precautions to avoid crime:

- Don't carry more cash than you need.
- Never leave valuables on the beach or by the pool.
- Always lock your car with any valuables out of sight in the boot.
- Beware of pickpockets in crowded markets or tourist sights.

Police assistance: ☎ 112 from any call box

ELECTRICITY

The power supply in Spain is 220–225 volts. Sockets accept two-round-pin style plugs. Visitors from the UK require an adaptor and US visitors a transformer for appliances operating on 100–120 volts.

OPENING HOURS

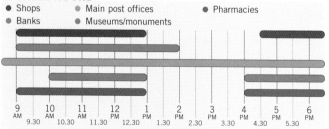

- Shops
- Banks
- Main post offices
- Museums/monuments
- Pharmacies

9 AM	10 AM	11 AM	12 PM	1 PM	2 PM	3 PM	4 PM	5 PM	6 PM
9.30	10.30	11.30	12.30	1.30	2.30	3.30	4.30	5.30	

Most shops close Saturday evening and all day Sunday, though supermarkets and shops in larger resorts may be open daily throughout the day. Banks open Saturday mornings in winter only. There is always one pharmacist on duty in the main towns; details are published in local papers and shop windows. Many museums close on Monday.

LANGUAGE

Although Spanish is still universally understood, it is Catalán that you are most likely to see and hear on the streets. It is spoken in Valencia, Andorra, the Balearic islands and parts of the French Pyrenees, as well as in Catalonia. Many Catalán words look like their equivalents in French or Spanish – but the sound of the language is utterly distinct.

hotel	*hotel*	bath/shower	*bany/dutxa*
campsite	*càmping*	washbasin/toilet	*lavabo/vàter*
apartment	*apartament*	balcony	*balcó*
single room	*habitació senzilla*	sea view	*vista al mar*
double room	*habitació doble*	one night	*una nit*
bank	*banc*	banknote	*bitllet de banc*
exchange bureau	*oficina de canvi*	credit card	*carta de crèdit*
cashier	*caixer*	change	*canvi*
travellers' cheque	*xec de viatge*	how much?	*quant és?*
foreign currency	*moneda estrangera*	post office	*correus*
breakfast	*esmorzar*	white wine/red wine	*vi blanc/vi negre*
lunch/dinner	*dinar/sopar*	water	*aigua*
menu/set menu	*carta/menú*	sparkling/still	*amb gas/sense gas*
waiter/waitress	*cambrer/cambrera*	beer	*cervesa*
airport/aeroplane	*aeroport/avió*	return	*anar i tornar*
station/train	*estació/tren*	taxi/car	*taxi/cotxe*
bus	*autobús*	garage	*garatge*
boat	*vaixell*	petrol station	*gasolinera*
ticket	*bitllet*	motorway	*autopista*
yes/no	*si/no*	welcome	*benvinguts*
please/thank you	*sisplau/gràcies*	open/closed	*obert/tancat*
hello/goodbye	*hola/adéu*	I don't understand	*no ho entenc*
good morning	*bon dia*	do you speak	*parla anglès?*
good afternoon	*bona tarda*	English?	
goodnight	*bona nit*	I don't speak	*no parlo català*
excuse me/sorry	*perdoni/ho sento*	Catalán	

Best places to see

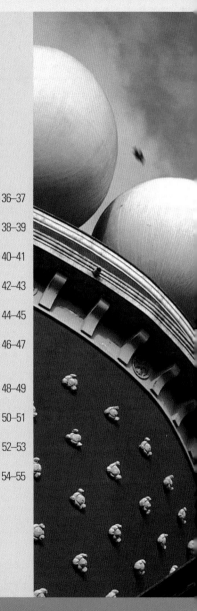

1 Besalú

A well-preserved medieval town centre at the heart of the region, with several Romanesque churches and the only Jewish bath house in Spain.

This small town at the confluence of the Fluvià and Capellada rivers was the historic capital of the Garrotxa region, ruled for more than 200 years by a dynasty established by Wilfred the Hairy. After the 12th century its importance declined, but following its declaration as a National Historic Monument in 1966 it has been restored to its former glory.

Come here on a Tuesday morning, when the porticoed central square, Plaça Llibertat, is buzzing with chatter and the market stalls are piled high with flowers, fruit and cheese, and you realize that this is still very much a working town. Along the cobbled streets which fan out from the square are delicatessens and antiques shops, set among medieval arches, columns and Gothic windows. Of several Romanesque churches, the most

impressive is the monastery church of Sant Pere, with a pair of stone lions adorning its façade.

The symbol of Besalú is its angled bridge over the Fluvià, built in the 11th century and destroyed several

times, most recently in the Spanish Civil War. Arriving by car, park on the Banyoles side and enter Besalú across the bridge. Near here is the Miqvé, the only remains of a once significant Jewish community. This ritual bathhouse, with thermal springs and running water from the river, was used by men before prayer and by women before marriage, childbirth and menstruation. The tourist office arranges guided visits.

✚ 5D 🍴 Choice of restaurants and cafés (€–€€) 🚌 From Figueres, Girona and Olot ❓ Market on Tue; Festa dels Dolors, evening procession on the Fri before Palm Sunday; *sardana* dancing on Easter Sunday; Festa Major, last weekend in Sep. A 1-hour miniature train tour in summer includes a guided walk and visit to Miqvé (moderate) ℹ Plaça Llibertat 1 ☎ 972 59 12 40

BEST PLACES TO SEE

2 Cadaqués

This fishing village and stylish resort has long attracted a curious mixture of artists, tourists and people seeking an alternative way of life.

Cadaqués appears at first sight to be a typical Mediterranean fishing village. It still is a fishing village, but it is much more than that. Picasso spent some time here in the early 20th century, but it was Salvador Dalí who really put Cadaqués on the map. His father came from here; it was here that he met his wife; and it was near here, at Portlligat, that he eventually settled down, attracted by the light, the remoteness and the rugged beauty of Spain's most easterly village.

There are reminders of Dalí everywhere: a statue on the seafront, a sundial on the façade of a hotel, the logo of the L'Hostal bar. In the 1960s, when hippies and intellectuals flocked to Dalí's side, Cadaqués was known as Spain's St Tropez. It holds the same appeal for many people today.

There are several art galleries and stylish boutiques. The **Museu de Cadaqués** features contemporary Catalán artists. The old town of steep and narrow streets winds its way from the waterfront up to the church of Santa Maria, with its baroque reredos.

➕ 11C 🍴 Wide choice of restaurants and bars (€–€€)
🚌 From Figueres and Roses ❓ Market on Mon; Mare de
Déu del Carme, procession of fishing boats on 16 Jul;
international music and arts festival, Jul and Aug
ℹ️ Carrer Cotxe 2A ☎ 972 25 83 15

Museu de Cadaqués
✉️ Carrer Narcís Monturiol 15 ☎ 972 25 88 77 🕐 Hours
vary according to exhibition. Usually, summer 10:30–1:30,
4–8 ✋ Moderate

3 Castell Gala Dalí

The castle which Salvador Dalí bought as a refuge for his wife has become a shrine to her memory and to the couple's bizarre relationship.

When Salvador and Gala Dalí were in exile in Italy during the Spanish Civil War, the painter promised his wife that he would one day buy her a castle. Thirty years later, he acquired this Gothic and Renaissance castle in the village of Púbol. Dalí wanted Gala to be able to get away from him, with her lovers if necessary, and insisted that he would never enter the castle without her permission.

The castle was in a state of disrepair and Dalí set about re-creating it. The result is a typically Dalíesque mixture of the grotesque, the beautiful and the absurd. Classical statues in the garden share space with elephant figures sculpted from cement; 17th-century tapestries hang beside *trompe l'oeil* painted radiators and huge Dalí canvases. Everywhere you look there are portraits of Gala, and her initial G is frequently worked into the design.

Gala spent little time in her castle, arriving for short stays each summer but continuing to live with Dalí in Portlligat. When she died in 1982, her body was driven to Púbol and buried in the crypt – with a stuffed giraffe looking on. Dalí moved into her room, but two years later he set fire to the bed and, despite a life-saving operation, he was never to

return to the castle. The Cadillac in which he insisted on leaving Púbol – he refused to take an ambulance – still sits in the garage. Dalí left the castle to the Spanish state and it was opened to the public as a museum in 1996.

✠ 20G ☎ 972 48 86 55 🕐 15 Jun–15 Sep daily 10–8; 15 Mar–14 Jun, 16 Sep–1 Nov Tue–Sun 10–6; 2 Nov–31 Dec Tue–Sun 10–5 💲 Moderate 🍴 Can Bosch (€) in village 🚌 Buses between Girona and Palafrugell pass 2km (1.2 miles) away

4 Empúries

An ancient Greek and Roman settlement on the shores of the Gulf of Roses, where Spain first came into contact with wider European culture.

It was the Greeks who first established a trading post *(emporion)* here on what was then an island; contact between Greek settlers and indigenous tribes led to the development of the Iberian culture. The Romans anchored at Empúries in 218BC, the first step on the route to the colonization of Spain. The Roman city of Emporiae was abandoned in the 3rd century AD and only rediscovered by archaeologists in 1908. Much of it has still to be excavated.

The remains of the Roman city show how much Spanish town planning owes to Roman influence. The forum at the centre, the forerunner of the Plaça Major, would once have been surrounded by

arcades; there were temples at one end and a main street leading to the city walls. Even the amphitheatre outside the walls has its equivalent in today's bullring or football stadium.

Below is the Greek city, dominated by a statue of

Asklepios, the god of healing (the original is in Barcelona's archaeological museum). A small museum interprets the ruins, and there is an excellent audiovisual show. Afterwards you can walk along the seafront, past the original Greek jetty, to the village of Sant Martí d'Empúries, site of the first Greek settlement.

✚ 10E ✉ 1km (0.5 miles) north of L'Escala ☎ 972 77 02 08 🕓 Jun–Sep daily 10–8; Oct–May daily 10–6. Closed 1 Jan, 25 Dec ✋ Inexpensive; extra charge for audiovisual show 🍴 Snack bar (€) on site, restaurants (€–€€) in Sant Martí d'Empúries 🚌 To L'Escala from Figueres, Girona and Palafrugell

5 Girona Old Town

The restoration of the old quarter at the heart of Girona has been one of the great success stories of modern Catalonia.

As recently as 1964, the British travel writer Jan Morris described Girona as 'a shabby city of the north', but nobody could say that today. The political and cultural renaissance since 1980 has been accompanied by an architectural revival and a determination to show this historic city at its best. Dilapidated convents have been given new life as museums and art galleries; the university has been restored to its 16th-century home, and the narrow streets of the medieval Jewish district, the Call Jueu (➤ 84), have been carefully restored.

This is a city for strolling, wandering at random among the maze of streets and going wherever a hidden archway or flight of steps leads you. Sun and shade, iron and stone, courtyards and balconies, narrow alleys and wide open squares, all come together here in perfect harmony.

Girona is at its most enchanting in the streets of the old guilds. Between Plaça de l'Oli and Plaça del Vi, once the oil and wine markets, lies a network of narrow lanes, each named after a medieval trade. Carrer de l'Argenteria was once lined with silversmiths, Carrer de Mercaders with merchants, Carrer de les Ferreries Velles with blacksmiths and Carrer Peixateries Velles with fishmongers. Their places may have been taken by trendy cafés and boutiques, but the streets are still appealing.

➕ *Girona 6d*
🍴 Choice of restaurants and cafés (€–€€€)
🚌 Girona bus station, 1km (0.5 miles) away
🚆 Girona, 1km (0.5 miles) away
❓ Holy Week procession on Good Friday
ℹ️ Rambla de la Llibertat 1
☎ 972 22 65 75

6 Monestir de Sant Pere de Rodes

Some claim that the monastery was built on the site of a Roman temple, but the more colourful story concerns Pope Boniface IV (608–615) and St Peter's head. With Rome under threat, the Pope ordered the church's most sacred relics to be sent to Spain for safe-keeping. When the time came to retrieve them, the head was nowhere to be found, so a monastery was built on the site here and dedicated to the saint. There are records of a monastery here from AD878 – though recent excavations suggest that the site was in use long before that. The present church, dating from 1022, marks the transition to Romanesque architecture in Catalonia. The original cloister, its galleries decorated with murals, is covered by an upper cloister on the same level as the church. This was an important place of pilgrimage throughout the Middle Ages, but fell into decline after the 14th century. The last monks left in 1798.

There are good views of the monastery from the chapel of Santa Elena, all that remains of the village which grew up around the church. For the best views, climb the path behind

the monastery to the ruined castle of
Sant Salvador. Look down over the
monastery and out to sea, then turn
to see the Pyrenees on the horizon.
The sunrises up here – some of the
first in Spain – are magical.

✚ 10C ☎ 972 38 75 59 🕒 Jun–Sep
Tue–Sun 10–7:30; Oct–May Tue–Sun 10–5
✋ Moderate (free on Tue) 🍴 Café-
restaurant (€) 🚌 El Port de la Selva (5km/
3 miles) 🚉 Vilajuïga (8km/5 miles)

7

Parc Natural de l'Aiguamolls de l'Empordà

This wetland nature reserve provides a refuge for wildlife and migrant birds and a peaceful haven for visitors escaping from the crowded beaches.

Once upon a time, marshes covered the coastal plain; Empúries (➤ 42–43) was an island and the Montgrí mountains were surrounded by fens. As the population grew, the marshes disappeared, at first as a result of agriculture and lately because of tourism. The building of the marina on former

marshland at Empúria-brava
(➤ 139), galvanized
environmentalists into action,
leading to the creation of this
natural park in 1983.

Carp, mullet and eel thrive in
the lakes; there are badgers,
newts and voles, and otters
are being reintroduced. Above all the Empordà
marshes are an important refuge for aquatic and
migrant birds. Herons, ducks and geese live on the
ponds; other species that breed here include the
stone-curlew and the black-winged stilt. This is
Spain's only nesting ground for the garganey, a
rare species of duck. Seabirds flock here in winter,
and during the main migrant seasons (Mar to May
and Aug to Oct), it is possible to see 100 species
in a day.

At the information centre in **El Cortalet** you can
pick up leaflets and maps, and hire out binoculars,
field guides and wheelchairs. There are two easy,
waymarked trails from here, with hides overlooking
the lagoons; except during the nesting season
(April to mid-June) they can be combined with a
walk along the beach in a two-hour circular trail.

✚ 9D
El Cortalet
✉ Off the road from Castelló d'Empúries to Sant Pere
Pescador ☎ 972 45 42 22 🕓 Trails open at all times
💷 Free (charge for car parking) 🚌 Castelló d'Empúries
❓ Keep to paths; be prepared for flooding in winter
ℹ Apr–Sep 9:30–2, 4:30–7; Oct–Mar 9:30–2, 3:30–6.
Closed 1 Jan, 25 Dec

8 Roses

**A fishing port and ancient
Greek colony, Roses
has become the tourist capital
of the northern Costa Brava.**

With 4km (2.5 miles) of sandy beach
at the head of a great sweeping bay,
Roses is the perfect setting for a
bucket-and-spade holiday. The
sheltered waters are ideal for
watersports, with windsurfing, sailing
and waterskiing all available. There are
also several smaller coves, beginning
with Canyelles and Almadrava, 3km
(2 miles) beyond the fishing harbour to the southeast. A hair-
raising drive across a rugged landscape leads to the remote
creek of Cala Montjoi; on the way you pass the Creu d'en
Cobertella, the largest prehistoric burial chamber in Catalonia,
dating from 3000BC.

Roses was founded in
the 8th century BC by
Greek settlers, who
named it Rhodes after
their homeland, but it
was the Romans who
developed the fishing
industry which led to the
town's wealth. It is still
an important fishing
port. With 50 hotels, five
campsites and dozens of
restaurants and bars, it
is a little too lively for
some; but if you want a

traditional beach holiday, with easy access to the quieter north coast, this is the best place.

The star-shaped **Ciutadella** (Citadel) at the entrance to town is a 16th-century fortress on the site of the original Greek city, with Roman and medieval remains within its walls – you can clamber over the ruins and look down into the moat. Another ruined castle, east of town, stands on the slopes of Puig Rom hill. Climb this hill at sunset for romantic views over the Bay of Roses with the snow-capped Pyrenees in the distance.

✚ 10C 🍴 Wide choice of restaurants and cafés (€–€€€) 🚌 From Cadaqués and Figueres 🚢 Trips to Cadaqués and Cala Montjoi in summer ❓ Market on Sun; Mare del Déu del Carme, procession of fishing boats on 16 Jul

ℹ Avinguda de Rhode 77 ☎ 972 15 05 37

Ciutadella de Roses

🕐 Apr–Sep daily 10–8, Oct–Mar Tue–Sun 10–6

✋ Inexpensive

9 Teatre-Museu Dalí

The memorial which Salvador Dalí created for himself in his home town of Figueres is a journey through the imagination of a tortured genius.

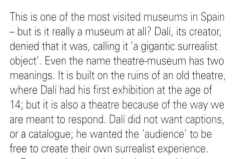

This is one of the most visited museums in Spain – but is it really a museum at all? Dalí, its creator, denied that it was, calling it 'a gigantic surrealist object'. Even the name theatre-museum has two meanings. It is built on the ruins of an old theatre, where Dalí had his first exhibition at the age of 14; but it is also a theatre because of the way we are meant to respond. Dalí did not want captions, or a catalogue; he wanted the 'audience' to be free to create their own surrealist experience.

From outside the view is dominated by the transparent dome on the roof, together with Dalí's trademark eggs on the façade. Once inside, you are drawn to the courtyard, with its central sculpture, *Rainy Taxi*, featuring a giant model of Dalí's wife Gala standing on a black Cadillac. Some things you cannot miss – like the Mae West room, where a sofa and two fireplaces are turned by means of a lens into a pouting face. Sooner or later you reach the crypt, where Dalí is buried; Dalí spent his last years in the Torre Galatea, and on his deathbed told the Mayor of Figueres he wanted to be buried in his theatre, rather than with Gala in her castle at Púbol. A separate exhibition dedicated to Dalí's jewellery is now open.

🚌 8C ✉ Plaça Gala-Salvador Dalí 5, Figueres ☎ 972 67 75 00 🕐 Jul–Sep daily 9–7:15; Oct–Jun Tue–Sun 10:30–5:15; closed 1 Jan, 25 Dec 💷 Expensive
🚌 Figueres bus station, 1km (0.5 miles) away
❓ Night-time opening in Aug, 10–12:30 🚉 Figueres, 1km (0.5 miles) away

10 Tossa de Mar

The remains of a fortified medieval village look down on a horseshoe beach, making Tossa the most attractive of the Costa Brava resorts.

One resort on the crowded southern coast stands out head and shoulders above its neighbours. The beach alone would be enough to draw visitors, with safe swimming and sheltered sunbathing in an idyllic bay, and several smaller coves within easy reach. But what makes Tossa special is its walled medieval village (Vila Vella), standing proudly above the bay as it has done for more than 800 years.

Climb up from the main beach, Platja Gran, pausing to glance back at the sea through the arched window of an abandoned church, and you soon reach this attractive village. It was established in 1186 by the Abbot of Ripoll on the promontory of Mont Guardí. Beneath here, just behind the beach, is the Vila Nova (New Town), a warren of back streets and 19th-century houses around the parish church.

Tossa was one of the first places on the Costa Brava to attract foreign visitors. The painter Marc Chagall spent the summer of 1934 here and called it his 'blue paradise'. The **Museu Municipal,** in the former Abbot's palace, contains letters from Chagall, who was delighted that the museum was to display one of his paintings. Also worth a visit is the Mediterranean Lighthouse Interpretation Centre in the old lighthouse.

✚ 20L 🍴 Restaurants/cafés (€–€€) 🚌 From Lloret de
Mar (and from Girona in summer) 🚢 South coast resorts
in summer ❓ Market Thu
ℹ️ Avinguda del Pelegrí 25 ☎ 972 34 01 08
Museu Municipal
✉️ Plaça Roig i Soler 1 ☎ 972 34 07 09 🕐 Oct–May
Tue–Sat 10–2, 4–6, Sun 10–2; Jun–Sep daily 10–8
✋ Inexpensive

Best things to do

Good places to have lunch

Abril (€)

Healthy four-course lunch menu served at outdoor tables.

✉ Carrer de Santa Clara 27, Girona

☎ 972 411055

Boira (€–€€)

Tapas downstairs as well as an upstairs restaurant with romantic views over the river.

✉ Plaça Independència 17, Girona

☎ 972 21 96 05.

Can Salvi (€€–€€€)

Fishy specialities on the seafront promenade.

✉ Passeig del Mar 23, Sant Feliu de Guíxols ☎ 972 32 10 13

Cap de Creus (€–€€)

Fish, salads and curries in a fabulous setting.

✉ Cap de Creus ☎ 972 19 90 05

Curia Reial (€€)

Hearty meat dishes and 'volcanic cuisine' served on a terrace overlooking the medieval bridge.

✉ Plaça Llibertat, Besalú

☎ 972 59 02 63

Durán (€€)
Top-notch Catalán cooking in Salvador Dalí's old haunt.
✉ Carrer Lasauca 5, Figueres ☎ 972 50 12 50

El Port (€–€€€)
Fresh fish from the neighbouring market beneath the harbour walls.
✉ Esplanada del Port, Blanes ☎ 972 33 48 19

La Riera (€)
Hearty Catalán cooking at sensible prices in a village known for its food.
✉ Plaça de les Voltes 3, Peratallada ☎ 972 634142

Santa Marta (€€)
Fish restaurant inside the Vila Vella.
✉ Carrer Francesc Aromir 2, Tossa de Mar ☎ 972 340472

Tragamar (€€)
Stylish *tapas* and Catalán cuisine right beside the beach.
✉ Platja del Canadell, Calella de Palafrugell ☎ 972 61 51 89

Top activities

Diving and snorkelling: especially around the Illes Medes (Medes Islands; ➤ 100).

Fishing: licences for sea-fishing are issued by the local tourist offices.

Golf: there are ten courses in the Costa Brava (➤ 72–73).

Horse-back riding: there are centres in most of the main resorts, with tuition for beginners and more advanced riders.

Sailing: there are 17 marinas between Blanes and Portbou, ranging from Aiguablava (62 moorings) to Empúria-brava (4,000 moorings). See also ➤ 76–77.

Skiing: La Molina and Vall de Núria are popular winter sports centres in the Pyrenees, near Ripoll.

Swimming: the Costa Brava's beaches are perfect for safe swimming.

Walking: on the GR92 coastal path, or inland in the volcanic Garrotxa region or the Albera mountain range.

Waterskiing: equipment rental and tuition are available at all of the main resorts.

Windsurfing: all along the coast, and especially around the Gulf of Roses.

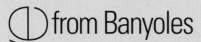

a drive from Banyoles

This drive takes you into the heart of the Garrotxa, the region of dormant volcanoes just inland from Banyoles.

Start by the sports stadium on Carrer Alfonso XII, between central Banyoles and the lake, and take the main road heading north with the lake on your left.

After 4km (2.5 miles) this road merges with the C66 from Girona. Almost immediately you see the high peaks of the Pyrenees up ahead in the distance. Soon you reach Besalú (► 36–37): to explore this delightful town, park on the right, walk down to the riverbank and follow the signs to enter Besalú across the medieval Pont Vell.

Leaving Besalú, continue on the main road towards Olot.

This soon becomes the A26 road. When you see a tunnel ahead, take the exit on to the old N260 to Castellfollit de la Roca (► 98–99), perched on a ridge to your left.

Continue through this village and rejoin the A26. When the road ends, turn left towards Olot and keep left to skirt the city centre, following signs to Santa Pau.

Shortly after turning on to the Santa Pau road, you see the Can Serra car park and information centre on your left. If you have time, you could stop here and do the walk described on pages 106–107.

Continue on this winding road to Santa Pau (➤ 111). After exploring the village, return to the same road as it twists down to the plain, with lovely views all the way.

Eventually you arrive at Banyoles beside the lake.

Distance 76km (47 miles)
Time 2 hours plus stops along the way
Start/end point Banyoles ✚ 6E
Lunch Cal Sastre (€€) ✉ Placeta dels Balls 6, Santa Pau
☎ 972 68 04 21

Top souvenir ideas

Burro català: the 'Catalán donkey' has become a self-mocking symbol of Catalonia, seen on car stickers and T-shirts as an alternative to the Spanish bull.

Caganer: literally a 'defecator', this uniquely Catalán nativity figure is placed in Christmas crib scenes alongside the shepherds and Holy Family.

Carnival masks: come here in February and the shops are full of masks depicting *dimoni* (devils) and giants.

Catalán flag: the red and gold stripes of the Catalán flag are a powerful symbol of national identity.

Dalí art: Salvador Dalí's surreal designs on posters, prints and T-shirts make a colourful souvenir.

Fuet: this salami-type sausage from Vic makes a delicious treat to take home, along with others such as *llonganissa*.

Havaneres: these traditional Caribbean sea shanties are sung in Calella de Palafrugell and are also available on CD.

Olive oil: the best is Dauro de l'Empordà, produced from Arbequina olives in Siurana.

Pottery: visit La Bisbal for a wonderful array of local ceramics, from simple cooking pots to bright, arty designs.

Wine: choose from sparkling Catalán *cava* or the Costa Brava's own Vi de l'Empordà.

Best beaches

- Blanes (➤ 158–159)

- Empúria-brava (➤ 139)

- L'Estartit (➤ 99)

- Lloret de Mar (➤ 162–165)

Places to take the children

Aquabrava

Waterslides, beaches and the biggest wave pool in Europe are among the attractions on offer.

✉ Carretera de Cadaqués, Roses ☎ 972 25 43 44 🕓 Jun–Sep daily 10–7 🚌 Free bus from Roses and Empúria-brava

Aquadiver

Children who enjoy messing about in water will love this – wave machines, zigzagging toboggans, safe white-water rapids and a 'kamikaze' free-fall ride.

✉ Carretera Circumval lació, Platja d'Aro ☎ 972 82 82 83 🕓 Jun–Sep daily 10–6 (Jul–Aug 10–7) 🚌 Free bus from Platja d'Aro, Palamós and Sant Feliu de Guíxols

Gnomo Park

Little children will love this 'gnome farm', which offers mini-golf, an adventure playground, train rides, a woodland trail – and gnomes! ✉ Carretera de Lloret, near Blanes ☎ 972 36 80 80 🕓 Easter–Oct Tue–Sun 11–9; Nov–Easter Sat–Sun 11–9

Magic Park

Funfair and indoor play area with roller-skating, a miniature boating

lake, inflatable toys, dodgem cars, a carousel, video games and a soft play area for younger children. There is another Magic Park in Lloret de Mar. ✉ Avinguda S'Agaró 86, Platja d'Aro ☎ 972 81 78 64 🕓 Daily 10am–1am

Marineland

Aquatic park with dolphin and sea lion shows and a small zoo with penguins and seals. Thrill rides include the Black Hole, Boomerang, Kamikaze and Twister. Separate pools and rides for the under-6s; picnic area among the pine trees.

✉ Carretera Malgrat a Palafolls, near Blanes ☎ 937 65 48 02 ⊕ May–Sep daily 10–6 (Jul–Aug 10–7) 🚍 Free bus from Blanes, Lloret de Mar and Tossa de Mar

Museu Fauna Salvatge

Conjure up the sounds and sights of Pyrenean wildlife at the touch of a button at this interactive 'zoo'.

✉ Carrer Dr Zamenhoff, Olot ☎ 972 27 26 49 ⊕ Daily 9–9

The Nautilus Adventure

Children will enjoy any boat trip on the Costa Brava, but this one is extra-special as it travels out to the Medes Islands in boats with submerged cabins, allowing you to observe the fish swimming along the seabed.

✉ Passeig Marítim 23, L'Estartit ☎ 972 75 14 89 ⊕ Departures several times a day in summer and at winter weekends, depending on the weather.

Parc Animal de Sobrestany

Wildlife park with deer, bison, wild boar, ostriches and Pyrenean sheep. There is a walking trail and a driving tour where you are given a bag of feed for the animals.

✉ Camí de Sobrestany, between Torroella de Montgrí and L'Escala ☎ 972 78 84 94 ⊕ Daily 9–8 summer, 10–6 winter

Water World

Pools, slides and the Water Mountain, where you can take a big-dipping roller-coaster ride.

✉ Carretera Vidreres, Lloret de Mar ⊕ May–Sep, daily 10–6 (Jul–Aug 10–7) ☎ 972 36 86 13 🚍 Free bus from Blanes, Lloret de Mar and Tossa de Mar

Great coastal views

Cap de Creus (► 136)

Cap Roig, Calella de Palafrugell (► 96–97)

Cap de Sant Sebastià, Llafranc (► 101)

Castell de Begur, Begur (► 94)

Castell del Montgrí, Toroella de Montgrí (► 113)

Castell de Sant Joan, Blanes (► 159)

Castell de Sant Salvador, above Monestir de Sant Pere de Rodes (► 47)

Ermita de Sant Elm, Sant Feliu de Guíxols (► 169)

Puig Rom, Roses (► 51)

Tossa de Mar to Sant Feliu de Guíxols – views from the belvederes along the coastal corniche (► 54–55)

Golf courses

CENTRAL COSTA BRAVA
Club de Golf Girona

✉ Sant Julià de Ramis, near Girona ☎ 972 171641

Empordà Golf Club

✉ Gualta, near Torroella de Montgrí ☎ 972 760450

Golf Platja de Pals
 Platja de Pals ☎ 972 667739

Golf Serres de Pals
Platja de Pals ☎ 972 637375

THE NORTH COAST AND BEYOND
Peralada Golf Club
Peralada ☎ 972 538287

Torremirona Golf Club
Navata, between Figueres and Besalú ☎ 972 553737

THE SOUTH COAST AND BEYOND
Club de Golf Costa Brava
Santa Cristina d'Aro, near Platja d'Aro ☎ 972 837150

Club de Golf d'Aro-Masnou
Platja d'Aro ☎ 972 826900

L'Àngel de Lloret
Lloret de Mar ☎ 972 368533

PGA Golf de Catalunya
Caldes de Malavella ☎ 972 472577

Best small towns and villages

Begur: a pretty hilltop town crowned by a ruined castle (► 94)

Besalú: a beautifully restored historic capital, preserved as an open-air museum (► 36–37)

Cadaqués: this chic Catalán fishing village has become a shrine to Salvador Dalí (► 38–39)

Calella de Palafrugell: an enjoyable, old-style seaside resort with restaurants on the beach (► 96–97)

Castelló d'Empúries: an unassuming county town with a magnificent parish church (► 138–139)

Pals: a showpiece village of Gothic and medieval architecture
(➤ 108)

Peratallada: a fortified medieval village with stone bridges,
archways and cobbled streets (➤ 108)

Sant Pere Pescador: a laid-back riverside town with a splendid
unspoiled beach (➤ 146–147)

Santa Pau: a fortified village at the heart of the volcanic Garrotxa
region (➤ 111)

Torroella de Montgrí: an attractive market town in the shadow
of a 13th-century castle (➤ 112–113)

Best marinas

The Costa Brava is a popular stopping-off point for yachting folk, sailing around the Mediterranean. The following marinas all have mooring and repair services, though it is essential to book well ahead for facilities during the summer months. It is also possible to charter yachts at most of these ports or book short trips.

Aiguablava
62 moorings ☎ 972 62 24 49

Blanes
320 moorings ☎ 972 33 05 52

Cala Canyelles (Lloret de Mar)
130 moorings ☎ 972 36 88 18

Colera
150 moorings ☎ 972 38 90 95

Empúria-brava
4,000 moorings ☎ 972 45 12 39

L'Escala
825 moorings ☎ 972 77 00 16

L'Estartit
738 moorings ☎ 972 75 14 02

Llafranc
140 moorings ☎ 972 30 07 54

Llançà
500 moorings ☎ 972 38 07 10

Palamós
867 moorings ☎ 972 60 10 00

Platja d'Aro
830 moorings ☎ 972 81 89 29

El Port de la Selva
328 moorings ☎ 972 38 70 00

Portbou
250 moorings ☎ 972 39 06 34

Roses
467 moorings ☎ 972 15 44 12

Sant Feliu de Guíxols
260 moorings ☎ 972 32 17 00

Santa Margarida (Roses)
1,100 moorings ☎ 972 25 77 00

Exploring

When tourists started visiting Spain in the 1950s, it was to the Costa Brava that they came. Other, bigger costas followed, but it was this small corner near the French border led the way. Fishing villages were transformed almost overnight into high-rise resorts; the face of the coastline changed more in a generation than in the previous thousand years. The Costa Brava virtually invented the sun-and-sea holiday.

Yet those rocky creeks still exist. There are villas climbing up the hillsides now, but this is still recognizable as Agulló's Wild Coast. There are areas of unspoiled marshland, Greek and Roman ruins and long, sandy beaches with not a hotel in sight. The main town, Girona, has a charming, medieval heart, and further inland are solid Catalán towns like Olot and Vic.

The Costa Brava is changing its image – no longer cheap and cheerful, but chic, confident and cool.

Girona and Central Costa Brava

The craggy coastline of cliffs, coves and cork woods at the heart of the Costa Brava epitomizes the nature of the 'Wild Coast'. Tourism has arrived here, but slowly – there are few high-rise hotels, and the villas on the hillsides are mostly second homes for the people of Barcelona. The tranquil resorts around Begur and Palafrugell, with their sandy beaches and shimmering bays, are some of the most relaxing places on the entire Catalán coast.

Girona

Inland, towns like Besalú and Pals have been restored to their medieval splendour, while the Garrotxa region of sleeping volcanoes around Olot makes for an interesting day out. There are historic castles and monasteries to be explored, and Girona, the provincial capital, is one of the most pleasing cities in Spain.

GIRONA

The capital of the Costa Brava region was founded by the Romans on the site of an Iberian settlement in the 1st century BC. Over the years it has been subject to numerous invasions, including Charlemagne in 785 and Napoleon in 1809. The city you see today consists of a medieval centre built on top of the Roman foundations, and an expanding new town across the Onyar River.

You can still make out traces of the old Roman city. Carrer de la Força, the cobbled street at the heart of the Jewish quarter, was once part of the Roman Via Augusta, a continental highway linking Rome to southern Spain. The Sobreportes arch at the foot of the cathedral steps is built over one of the old Roman entrances to the city. The statue of the Virgin of Good Death standing in a niche above the arch is a reminder that in later times prisoners were led through this gate to their execution.

But modern Girona is about more than ancient monuments. It's a thriving university city and a lively provincial capital. The city has been called Barcelona's little sister. It has all the style of the Catalán capital, but is more intimate and approachable.

✚ 19H

🛈 Rambla de la Llibertat 1 ☎ 972 22 65 75

Banys Àrabs

The so-called Arab Baths are a 13th-century Romanesque creation, based on an earlier Moorish design and influenced by Roman styles. They are one of the best preserved medieval bath houses in Spain. The most impressive room is the apodyterium or changing-room, with an octagonal pool at its centre beneath a domed skylight supported by eight columns. From here you can walk through the frigidarium (cold chamber) and tepidarium (warm bath) to reach the caldarium, an early sauna with underground heating.

✚ *Girona 7b* ✉ Carrer del Rei Ferran el Catòlic ⚙ Apr–Sep Mon–Sat 10–7, Sun 10–2; Oct–May daily 10–2. Closed 1 Jan, 6 Jan, Easter Sunday, 26–26 Dec 💷 Inexpensive

Call Jueu

For six centuries until their expulsion in 1492, Girona was home to one of the largest Jewish communities in Spain. At one time up to 1,000 Jews lived in the area around Carrer de la Força, where there were three synagogues, a Jewish school, a ritual bath and a Jewish butcher.

At the centre of the Jewish ghetto is the Centre Bonastruc Ça Porta. This Jewish museum and cultural centre is named after the founder of the Cabbalist school of Judaism, also known as Rabbi Nahmánides, who was born in Girona in 1194. Cabbalism is a secret system of mysticism, metaphysics and mathematics which claims to read hidden messages into the scriptures. The **Museu d'Història dels Jueus** tells the tragic story of Catalonia's Jews, persecuted for 300 years before being finally driven out. Centuries later, this small centre in Girona is providing a focus for the renaissance of Jewish Spain.

✚ *Girona 7c* 🍴 El Pou del Call, Carrer de la Força 14 (€€)

Museu d'Història dels Jueus

✉ Carrer de la Força 8 ☎ 972 21 67 61 🕒 May–Oct Mon–Sat 10–8, Sun 10–3; Nov–Apr Mon–Sat 10–6, Sun 10–3 🎫 Inexpensive

Catedral

Girona's cathedral is one of the great churches of Spain. Begun in 1312 on the site of an earlier church (and before that a mosque), it has evolved over the succeeding centuries into a triumph of different architectural styles, coming together to create a unifying and satisfying whole.

The best way to approach the cathedral is via the huge rococo staircase leading up to its Renaissance façade, an exquisite piece of stone carving with floral reliefs and sculptures of saints supporting the central rose window. Inside, the cathedral is dominated by its single Gothic nave, at 23m (75ft) the widest in Europe. Other features to look out for include the 11th-century alabaster altarpiece (a remnant of the earlier church) and the embossed silver canopy above the high altar.

The Treasury contains an illustrated 10th-century manuscript of the *Beatus*, or Commentary on the Apocalypse and the 11th-century *Tapestry of the Creation*. The ticket also gives access to the 12th-century Romanesque cloisters, with a view of the original bell tower, Torre de Carlemany, skilfully incorporated into the 14th-century Gothic design.

🕂 *Girona 7b* ✉ Plaça de la Catedral ☎ 972 21 44 26 🕓 Apr–Oct daily 10–8; Nov–Mar daily 10–7 💷 Moderate (free on Sun). Ticket allows entry to the museum and cloisters. Audio-guide is also included in the price of the ticket ❓ Access through the main door is for services only; visitors enter through the side door.

a walk around Girona Old Town

This walk is best done during the early evening, when the citizens of Girona take their *passeig* along the Rambla.

Start at Pont de Pedra, the stone bridge to the north of Plaça de Catalunya. Cross this bridge to reach the old town and continue into the arcaded Plaça del Vi. Turn left and cross the square to reach Carrer dels Ciutadans.

At this point you could take one of the narrow alleys to your left to explore the medieval streets of the guilds (➤ 45).

Carrer dels Ciutadans leads into Plaça de l'Oli. Turn right to climb the steps towards the church of Sant Martí. Halfway up the steps, fork left beneath the arch formed by the façade of Palau dels Agullana, a handsome Gothic mansion. Continue climbing to reach Plaça Sant Domènec, dominated by its old university. Turn left to leave the square, then left again along Carrer dels Alemanys into Carrer Bellmirall.

Turn right and cross Plaça dels Lledoners to reach the cathedral's southern door. After visiting the cathedral, walk down the flight of steps beneath its main façade into Plaça de la Catedral.

Turn left along Carrer de la Força. This road, and the steep, dark alleys to its left, form the heart of the atmospheric Jewish quarter (➤ 84). Reaching a small square, descend the steps to your right, leading to Carrer de l'Argenteria.

This smart shopping street leads into the Rambla (➤ 92), where you can end your walk with *tapas* and a drink beneath the arches.

Distance 2km (1.2 miles)
Time 1 hour
Start/end point Pont de Pedra ✚ *Girona 6d* 🚌 1km (0.5 miles) from bus and railway stations
Tapas Café l'Arcada (€) ✉ Rambla de la Llibertat 38
☎ 972 20 10 15

Eixample

Most visitors to Girona spend all their time in the old town to the east of the River Onyar, but the Eixample ('extension'), on the other side of the river, is where most people live and work. Plaça de la Independència, where the old town meets the new, is a pleasant 19th-century arcaded square lined with restaurants, cafés and bars. The monument at the centre is to the defenders of Girona, under siege from Napoleon's troops in 1809. A short walk from here leads to the Parc de la Devesa, the city's playground and the largest urban park in Catalonia. Also near here is the **Museu del Cinema,** a fascinating collection of old cameras and cinematographic instruments.

Much of the new town was built in the early years of the 20th century, when the Modernist architectural movement was at its peak. Rafael Masó, born in Girona in 1880, was one of the leading figures in the movement. His Casa Teixidor, with its green ceramic lantern, can be seen on Carrer Santa Eugènia near the station. Designed as a warehouse with flats above, it is now a college of architecture.

✚ *Girona 5c* 🍽 Choice of restaurants and cafés (€–€€€) 🚌 Girona bus station is in this area 🚉 Girona station

Museu del Cinema

✉ Carrer Sèquia 1, Girona 🕿 972 41 27 77 🕔 May–Sep Tue–Sun 10–8; Oct–Apr Tue–Fri 10–6, Sat 10–8, Sun 11–3

Església de Sant Feliu

Girona's second church is easily recognized by its broken spire, damaged by lightning in 1581 and never repaired. It's an essential feature of the skyline when seen from the Onyar river. Built over the tomb of Feliu of Africa, a 4th-century Bishop of Girona, the church is a mix of architectural styles, from Romanesque to Gothic to baroque. Interesting features include the Roman sarcophagi, both pagan and Christian, built into the sanctuary walls, and the neo-classical chapel of Sant Narcís, with its marble walls and painted ceiling.

✚ *Girona 6b* ✉ Plaça de Sant Feliu 🕔 Variable 🖐 Free

Museu Arqueològic

This museum, in the 12th-century Romanesque monastery of Sant Pere de Galligants, contains an interesting collection of artefacts, from prehistoric to medieval times. Among the finds are Roman pottery and mosaics from Empúries (➤ 42–43) and three Roman milestones indicating the distance to Gerunda – the Roman name for the city. The cloister is notable for its beautifully sculpted capitals of mythological and biblical figures. The gardens around the back, with their shady fountains and views of the cathedral, would make a lovely spot for a siesta or a picnic.

✚ *Girona 7b* ✉ Plaça de Santa Llúcia
☎ 972 20 26 32 🕔 Jun–Sep Tue–Sat
10:30–1:30, 4–7, Sun 10–2; Oct–May Tue–Sat
10–2, 4–6, Sun 10–2 💷 Inexpensive

Museu d'Art

This museum in the former episcopal palace contains a large collection of Catalán art, from Romanesque to contemporary. Among the exhibits to look for are the 10th-century portable altar from the monastery of Sant Pere de Rodes (➤ 46–47), the 14th-century stencils used to design stained-glass windows for the cathedral in Girona, and the scenes of 20th-century Girona by the Catalán artist Santiago Rusinyol

and the Polish painter Mela Mutter.

🕂 *Girona 7c* ✉ Pujada de la Catedral 12 ☎ 972 20 38 34 🕐 Mar–Sep Tue–Sat 10–7, Sun 10–2; Oct–Feb Tue–Sat 10–6, Sun 10–2. Closed 1 Jan, 6 Jan, Easter Sunday, 25–26 Dec 🖐 Inexpensive

Museu d'Història de la Ciutat

The city museum, in the former Capuchin monastery of Sant Antoni, details the history of Girona from prehistoric times to today. Among the more unusual exhibits, the ground-floor display on industrial history features an old petrol pump, wireless sets and an early computer. Upstairs, there is a room devoted to the development of the *sardana* dance. The cemetery of the original convent is preserved just inside the entrance, with niches on the walls designed for mummified corpses.

🕂 *Girona 6c* ✉ Carrer de la Força 27 ☎ 972 22 22 29 🕐 Tue–Sat 10–2, 5–7, Sun 10–2 🖐 Inexpensive

Passeig de les Muralles

This walkway, along the medieval ramparts, offers marvellous views over the city. It begins near Plaça de Catalunya and continues past the convent and university of Sant Domènec to the ruined watchtower, Torre Gironella. For the best views, climb onto some of the newly restored towers, from where the distant peaks of the Pyrenees are visible on a clear day. The walk ends at Passeig Arqueològic, a series of attractively landscaped gardens between the cathedral and the River Galligants.

🕂 *Girona 8d* 🕐 Daily 8am–10pm 🖐 Free

Rambla and Riu Onyar

The Rambla beside the River Onyar is the hub of Girona's social life, and the best place to see it all is from one of the cafés beneath the vaulted arches. The Pont de Pedra, the stone bridge at the top of the Rambla, looks down over the river, with its iron and wooden bridges and brightly painted tenement houses backing on to the water. One of the bridges, the Pont de les Peixateries, cuts directly through the houses and on to the Rambla. It was built for the city by the French firm of Eiffel and Company, creators of the famous tower in Paris.

✚ *Girona 6d* 🍴 Several restaurants and cafés (€–€€) ❓ Flower market on Sat; Festa de Sant Jordi; book and flower market, 23 Apr

More to see in Central Costa Brava

AIGUABLAVA

It was here, in 1908, that the journalist Ferran Agulló first coined the term *costa brava*, and the rocky coves around Begur retain much of their ruggedness today. Of course they have now been discovered by tourists, and luxury 'urbanisations' are creeping up the hillsides, but out of season you can still have pine-fringed cliffs, golden sand and sparkling turquoise bays (Aiguablava means 'blue water') to yourself. The bay at Aiguablava is dominated, unusually, by an ugly white *parador*, a state-run hotel built on the cliffs to take advantage of the view. Across the bay is the chic resort of Fornells, little more than a marina, a smart hotel and a pair of tiny beaches. North of here are more small coves – Sa Riera, with views over the Medes islands, and Aiguafreda and Sa Tuna, linked by a footpath cut into the rock.

➕ 23H 🍴 Restaurants and bars at Aiguablava, Sa Riera and Sa Tuna (€€–€€€) 🚌 From Begur to Aiguablava, Aiguafreda and Fornells in summer

BANYOLES

The capital of the Pla de l'Estany county makes a pleasant place to while away a summer afternoon. The main square, Plaça Major, is a perfect example of the genre, with three- and four-storey houses climbing above the ground-floor arcades. Just outside Banyoles is a lake, fed by an underground spring, where the 1992 Olympic rowing contests and the 2004 World Championships were held. This is where the locals come to have fun in summer – you can swim, fish, rent a rowing boat or walk the 8km (5 miles) around the lake's shore. The jawbone of a pre-Neanderthal man, at least 100,000 years old, was discovered in 1887. A copy is kept in the **Museu Arqueològic,** housed in the 14th-century almshouses in the centre of town.

✚ 6E ❚❙ Restaurants (€–€€) 🚌 From Besalú, Girona and Olot

Museu Arqueològic

✉ Plaça de la Font 11 ☎ 972 57 23 61 🕐 Jul–Aug Tue–Sat 10:30–1:30, 4–7:30, Sun 10:30–2; Sep–Jun Tue–Sat 10:30–1:30, 4–6:30, Sun 10:30–2
💷 Inexpensive

BEGUR

This hilltop town with a ruined 15th-century castle makes a good base for exploring the rocky coves around Aiguablava (➤ 93). Narrow streets fan out from the church square, and you can climb to the castle for great views stretching north along the coastline as far as the Bay of Roses. Begur has grown in popularity and a rash of new holiday villas and apartments has contributed to a sense of urban sprawl, with fears that the medieval centre could be overwhelmed by development. Nevertheless, it remains a quiet and peaceful place, popular with Catalán weekenders.

✚ 23H ❚❙ Several restaurants and bars (€–€€) 🚌 From Girona and Palafrugell ❓ Market on Wed

BESALÚ

Best places to see, pages 36–37.

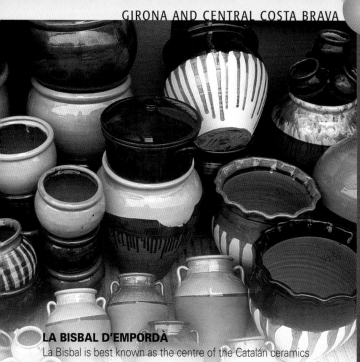

LA BISBAL D'EMPORDÀ

La Bisbal is best known as the centre of the Catalán ceramics industry. Its most abiding image – and the only one that many visitors see – is of the dozens of pottery shops lining Carrer de l'Aigüeta on the Girona road. There are good bargains to be had if you shop around, from simple glazed terracotta pots to innovative local designs. A twin-arched bridge, Pont Vell, leads over the River Daró into the centre of the old town, which comes alive each Friday with one of the region's busiest markets. Wander the narrow lanes and you keep coming across little surprises – a Gothic archway here, a fountain there, a shop selling hand-crafted wooden chairs or a shrine to the Virgin of Montserrat set high into a wall. The Romanesque bishops' palace, on the old town square, is a reminder that this quiet county town was once the seat of the bishops of Girona.

✚ 21H 🍴 Choice of restaurants and cafés (€–€€) 🚌 From Girona and Palafrugell ❓ Market on Fri

ℹ Plaça del Castell ☎ 972 64 51 66

CALELLA DE PALAFRUGELL

This pleasant resort consists of a series of coarse, sandy beaches strung out beneath an old fishing village. The village now includes a few whitewashed holiday villas, but it has lost none of its original

charm. You can still see working fishermen here, and fishing boats on the sand add a splash of colour to the scene. The people of Palafrugell and beyond head to Calella at weekends to eat at the waterfront seafood restaurants, while their children play on the beach.

Calella de Palafrugell is the setting for one of the Costa Brava's more unusual festivals each July, when popular musicians gather to sing *havaneres* on the beach. These melancholy sea shanties, brought back from Cuba by

Spanish sailors and rooted in the Creole music of the Caribbean, have been sung in the fishermen's taverns of Calella for at least 100 years. They are best enjoyed while drinking *cremat*, a local concoction of coffee, rum and cinnamon, which is served flambéed.

A cliff path from Calella leads around to the next bay at Llafranc (► 101). At the other end of the village, high above the bay, is the **Jardí Botànic de Cap Roig,** a beautiful garden laid out in 1927 by a White Russian emigré, Colonel Nicolai Woevodsky, and his English wife, Dorothy Webster. There are cypress, cork oak and mimosa trees and hundreds of Mediterranean plants, tall cedars and pine trees, bent by the wind and leaning towards the sea as if paying homage to the Mediterranean.

✚ 23H 🍴 Several beachside restaurants (€€) 🚌 From Palafrugell
❓ Festival of *havaneres*, first Sat in Jul

Jardí Botànic

✉ Cap Roig, 4km (2.5 miles) from village ☎ 972 61 45 82 🕐 Apr–Sep daily 9–8; Oct–Mar daily 9–6 👆 Moderate ❓ Costa Brava Jazz Festival held each Jul and Aug

CASTELL GALA DALÍ
Best places to see, pages 40–41.

CASTELLFOLLIT DE LA ROCA
Spectacularly perched on a 1km-long (0.6-mile) basalt promontory, carved out by the River Fluvià, this village looks for all the world as if it is about to fall off the cliff. The best view is from below, as you approach Castellfollit on the road from Besalú. At night, the cliff is floodlit and you can pick out the different geological layers in the

rock. The narrow streets of the village, their houses built from volcanic stone, converge by a church, where you can gaze 60m (195ft) down into the precipice below. Castellfollit is known for its almond biscuits and its pork sausages, and in the **Museu de l'Embotit** (Sausage Museum) you can taste the local products after looking at old-fashioned mincing machines and models of the *matança* or annual slaughter of pigs.

✚ 4D 🍴 Fonda Ca La Paula on main street (€) 🚌 From Besalú, Figueres, Girona and Olot

Museu de l'Embotit

✉ Carretera Girona 10 ☎ 972 29 44 63 🕐 Mon–Sat 9:30–1:30, 4–8, Sun 9:30–2, 4:30–8 ✋ Free

L'ESTARTIT

What was once little more than a fishing harbour, serving the nearby town of Torroella de Montgrí (➤ 112–113), has grown into a bustling, modern holiday resort with a reputation for nightlife and a thriving watersports industry. The main attraction here is the beach, which stretches for 5km (3 miles) and is backed by a seafront promenade. This is a good resort for families with young children – the water is shallow, the sand shelves gently and a miniature train trundles along the seafront. Unlike some of the larger resorts to the south, L'Estartit virtually closes down in winter, when all the locals retreat to Torroella de Montgrí. A popular attraction in summer is a boat trip to the Medes Islands (➤ 100), 1km (0.5 miles) offshore.

✚ 11F 🍴 Choice of restaurants and cafés (€–€€€) 🚌 From Girona and Torroella de Montgrí 🚢 Trips to Cadaqués and Palamós in summer ℹ Passeig Marítim ☎ 972 75 19 10

ILLES MEDES

Seven rocky islets, a continuation of the Montgrí massif, harbour a rich diversity of plant and animal life, and in 1985 they were declared Spain's first marine nature reserve. Local fishermen, banned from fishing in the area, feared for their livelihood; but the protection of the marine environment has been such a success that catches are up everywhere else as a result. Scuba divers come from all over Spain to swim among coral reefs and caves teeming with grouper, scorpion fish and spiny lobsters. Glass-bottomed boats leave regularly in summer from the harbour at L'Estartit (➤ 99); some trips include the opportunity to go snorkelling. There are strict regulations about fishing, boating and night diving in the protected area, and it is essential

to check with the authorities at the harbour in L'Estartit. In the past the islands have been used as a pirate hideout and a French military prison, but nowadays they are uninhabited – apart from the sea birds, especially the thousands of yellow-legged gulls, who breed here between March and May each year.

✚ 11F 🚢 Trips from L'Estartit in summer and occasionally on winter weekends

ℹ Carrer Eivissa, L'Estartit ☎ 972 75 11 03

LLAFRANC

Pine trees shade a beachfront promenade and yachts flutter in the small marina beside a perfect bay, where tamarisks grow out of the rocks around an arc of fine sand. Although this resort has grown more popular in recent years, the development is restrained and few of the buildings are more than two or three storeys high. A coastal path leads to Calella de Palafrugell (➤ 96–97), or you can walk or drive up to the lighthouse at Cap de Sant Sebastià for views back down over Llafranc.

✚ 23H 🍴 Several good restaurants (€€) 🚌 From Palafrugell ❓ Festival of *havaneres* on the beach, first Sat in Aug

OLOT

The capital of the Garrotxa region is a truly Catalán town which manages to be both industrious and stylish, conservative at heart with a radical edge. The people of Olot have a strong sense of Catalán identity: you are unlikely to hear anyone speaking Spanish. This Catalán spirit is openly displayed at the town's two biggest festivals – the *Aplec de la Sardana*, on the second Sunday in July, when visitors come from all over Catalonia to perform the *sardana* dance; and the *Festa de la Tura*, on 8 September, when figures of giants and hobby-horses parade through the streets.

Olot was a centre of textile production, and an art school was opened here in the 18th century. A century later, one of its pupils, Joaquim Vayreda, helped to found the Olot School of painters. The romantic scenes of rural life produced by these early Catalán impressionists were influenced by the European trends of the time, yet rooted in the Garrotxa landscape of volcanic hills.

The smart shopping streets of the old town around the Plaça Major lead to the neo-classical parish church of Sant Esteve. Near here is the start of the Rambla, also named Passeig Miquel Blay, after a well-known Olot sculptor. This delightful promenade, with coffee tables beneath the trees, contains some unusual Modernist architecture, as well as the 19th-century Teatre Principal. The Rambla is also the venue for Olot's lively market, which takes place on Monday mornings.

✚ 3E

🛈 Carrer del'Hospici 8 ☎ 972 26 01 41

Casal dels Volcans

The Garrotxa region around Olot has been at the centre of volcanic activity for hundreds of thousands of years. Although the most recent eruption was more than 11,000 years ago, the volcanoes are still considered dormant. Nor are volcanoes the only threat. A major earthquake struck the city in 1427, and there were tremors at nearby Besalú as recently as 1988. This museum, in the House of Volcanoes inside the botanic gardens at Parc Nou, explores the history and geology of the region, and its fauna and flora. The information centre for the Garrotxa natural park, in an office above the museum, is a good place to pick up leaflets about the area and walking maps and guides.

A waymarked walk (No 17) from the museum leads to the Volcà de Montsacopa, a typical volcano just north of the town centre. You can get there just as easily by following the signs from the Museu Comarcal, from where it will take around 20 minutes to reach the crater. Pass market gardens on the lower slopes, then walk uphill through an avenue of plane trees lined with Stations of the Cross. From the chapel of Sant Francesc, on the summit, there are marvellous views back down over Olot's rooftops and over the surrounding landscape, carved out by volcanic activity. You can walk right around the rim of the crater, or follow the path down to its floor. Another path leads to the crater of Volcà de la Garrinada, 500m (550yds) away.

✉ Avinguda de Santa Coloma (1km/0.6 miles from town)
☎ 972 26 67 62 🕐 Tue–Fri 10–2, 3–6, Sat 10–2, 4–7,
Sun 10–2 ✋ Inexpensive 🍴 Café

Museu Comarcal de la Garrotxa

An 18th-century hospice houses this county
museum of Garrotxa, with the most important
collection of work from the Olot School of
painters. Key figures in the movement were
Josep Berga i Boix (1837–1914) and Joaquim
Vayreda (1843–94). Many of Vayreda's paintings
of rural life are on display. The Modernist sculptor
Miquel Blay was also influenced by the Olot
School; among his works is a portrait of Berga i
Boix. More modern work includes nudes by
sculptor Josep Clarà, a pupil of Berga i Boix. The
museum also includes displays on Olot's
traditional industries – bell-making, clog-making,
textiles and religious statuary.

✉ Carrer de l'Hospici 8 ☎ 972 27 91 30 🕐 Tue–Fri
10–2, 3–6, Sat 10–2, 4–7, Sun 10–2 ✋ Inexpensive
🍴 Near by (€–€€) ❓ Combined entry ticket available
with Casal dels Volcans and Museu dels Sants

Museu Fauna Salvatge

One of Olot's tourist attractions is this
'interactive museum' above a petrol station on
the edge of town, where more than 10,000
species of Pyrenean bird and animal, together
with sound and light effects, can be summoned
to your computer screen at the touch of a button.
A good place to take the children on a rainy day.

✉ Carrer Dr Zamenhoff ☎ 972 27 26 49 🕐 Daily 9–9
✋ Inexpensive

a walk near Olot

This easy-to-follow walk provides an excellent introduction to the volcanic landscape around Olot and takes in three of its best-known features.

Start at the Can Serra car park, 5km (3 miles) out of Olot on the Santa Pau road. There is an information centre here where you can pick up a map of the walk. Take the underpass beneath the main road and descend the steps into the Fageda d'en Jordà beech wood.

The entire walk is waymarked with the symbol of two walkers on a red background accompanied by the number 1. The walk continues through this shady wood, joining a paved road to emerge beside a yoghurt factory before climbing sharply to the 11th-century church of Sant Miquel de Sacot.

Follow the waymarks. A short drop followed by a steep climb leads to the summit of the Santa Margarida volcano, from where an optional circular path heads down into the crater, with a small hermitage at its centre.

The path now descends to the main road, passing a farm where you can buy drinks and snacks.

Cross the road and take the lane which leads past the Santa Margarida restaurant, skirting the Volcà del Croscat. Until recently this volcano was quarried for its stone, and another optional path (No 15) leads to the scarred cliff-face to see the dramatic effects of the quarrying.

Continue around this volcano, and return through more beech woods to Can Serra.

Distance 10km (6 miles) plus optional extras
Time 3–4 hours
Start/end point Can Serra
Lunch Restaurant Santa Margarida (€) ✉ Opposite Lava campsite on the GI524 ☎ 972 68 02 70

PALAFRUGELL

A growing community of British expatriates has been attracted to this busy market town on the edge of the Lower Empordà plain. They are drawn to its down-to-earth Catalán atmosphere and to the excellent nearby beaches. It was once an important centre of cork production, and the Museu del Suro (cork museum) has some interesting displays on the history of the cork industry, as well as a selection of artefacts made from cork. The best time to visit Palafrugell is on Sunday, when the streets fill with stalls for one of the region's liveliest markets.

🛨 23H 🍴 Choice of restaurants (€–€€) 🚌 From Girona and nearby beaches
❓ Market on Sun; Spring Festival, Whit Sunday; annual festival, 19–21 Jul

PALS

This walled village of Gothic stone houses around a 15th-century castle was abandoned in 1939 after the Spanish Civil War, but was lovingly restored after 1948. Many of the houses are now second homes for people from Barcelona. At times the village is too pretty for its own good – numerous galleries and pottery shops testify to its popularity with tourists – and to appreciate it at its best you should come in the early morning or the evening, when the sunlight is at its most subtle and you can enjoy the alleys and archways without the crowds. The sandy beach of Platja de Pals, with its modern holiday facilities, is 5km (3 miles) away on the coast.

🛨 22G 🍴 Choice of restaurants and cafés (€€) 🚌 From Palafrugell

PERATALLADA

A bridge leads across the original moat to this medieval village, (the name means 'hewn stone'), and the cobbled alleyways are full of stone houses bearing ancient coats of arms. People travel for long distances at weekends to eat in Peratallada's restaurants, and to wander the back streets around the 11th-century castle.

🛨 22G 🍴 Choice of restaurants and cafés (€–€€€)

RIPOLL

Wilfred the Hairy, the first Count of Barcelona, used Ripoll as a base from which to unite the rival factions of the southern Pyrenees, following the reconquest of Catalonia from the Moors. He founded the **Monestir de Santa Maria** in 879 on the site of an earlier Visigothic church. During its golden age in the 11th and 12th centuries, the monastery ruled over an area stretching from Barcelona into modern France and became a great centre of European learning. Most of the church was destroyed by fire during the dissolution of the monasteries in 1835, but the great west portal survived. This is one of the jewels of Catalán Romanesque architecture, its pillars and arches covered in vivid reliefs of Biblical stories, zodiac signs and scenes from agricultural life. The 12th-century cloisters of the monastery church have also survived, with expressive faces on the sculpted capitals. The nearby Museu Etnogràfic has everything from matchboxes and cowbells to Civil War posters gathered together by a local historian.

🚩 1E (off map) 🍴 Restaurants and cafés (€–€€) 🚌 From Girona and Olot
❓ Market on Sat; wool festival, and farmer's wedding festival, May

Monestir de Santa Maria

✉ Plaça Abat Oliba 🕐 Daily 10–1, 3–7 ✋ Inexpensive

SANT JOAN DE LES ABADESSES

The convent here was established by Wilfred the Hairy as a gift
for his daughter Emma, whom he appointed the first abbess.
The 9th-century original has been replaced with a 12th-century
Romanesque church; its greatest treasure is its carved wooden
Calvary. Other sights in this attractive town, a good place to break
a journey between Ripoll and Olot, include a strangely pointed
bridge over the River Ter and the church of Sant Pol, with a tile
sculpture of *sardana* dancers among the ruins.

🚌 1D 🍴 Cafés and bars (€)
🚌 From Ripoll ❓ Market on
Sun

SANTA PAU

The tourist capital of the
Garrotxa region has at its
heart a fortified medieval
enclave with a well-restored
baronial castle. The centre
of the village is closed to
traffic, so it is best to park

outside and walk in through the original gateway, Portal Nou. Plaça
Major, the main square, is as attractive as any in Catalonia, with
wooden balconies, stone arcades and the Romanesque church
of Santa Maria. The castle, first built in the 14th century, is in the
neighbouring square, Placeta dels Balls. A short walk from here
is the Mirador Portal del Mar, giving panoramic views over the
Garrotxa valleys and a distant glimpse of the sea. Santa Pau is an
excellent base for exploring this volcanic region – you can follow
numerous well-marked footpaths, hire a mountain-bike or a horse,
take a ride in a horse-drawn carriage or fly over the volcanoes in
a helicopter or a balloon.

🚌 4E 🍴 Choice of restaurants (€–€€) 🚌 Occasional buses from Olot and
Banyoles ❓ For balloon flights contact Vol de Coloms ☎ 972 680255

TAMARIU

Named after the tamarisk trees that once surrounded its bay, Tamariu is the smallest and prettiest of the three resorts on this stretch of coastline near Palafrugell. In recent years it has become decidedly chic, and many of the old fishermen's cottages have been turned into holiday homes for Catalán families from Girona and Barcelona.

The main beach, a crescent of golden sand, is backed by a wide pedestrian promenade lined with seafood restaurants. A short walk around the headland to the north leads to the rocky cove of Aiguaxellida, with its own small beach.

➕ 23H 🍴 Seafood restaurants (€€–€€€) 🚌 From Palafrugell in summer
❓ Festival of *havaneres* on the beach, first Sat in Sep

TORROELLA DE MONTGRÍ

This delightful town of Gothic palaces, courtyards and narrow streets comes alive each Monday as the weekly market spills out in all directions from the porticoed main square, Plaça de la Vila. Stalls are piled high with local cheeses and sausages in this spot, where the *sardana*, the modern Catalán folk dance, was danced for the first time. The nearby **Can Quintana** cultural centre, housed in a historic mansion, contains the Museu de la Mediterrània, with interesting displays on local history, geology, wildlife and traditional music, as well as temporary art exhibitions. Recent archaeological excavations have revealed the presence of elephants, bears and rhinoceroses here in palaeolithic times. A steep climb from the town centre leads to the Castell del Montgrí, built in 1294 and recently restored, standing guard over the town on the limestone Montgrí massif.

🔲 10F 🍴 Cafés and bars in the town centre (€) 🚌 From L'Estartit, Figueres, Girona and Palafrugell ❓ Market on Mon; international music festival, Jul–Aug; Festa de Santa Caterina, Sun before 25 Nov

Can Quintana

✉ Carrer d'Ullà ☎ 972 75 51 8 🕐 Jul–Aug Mon–Sat 11–2, 6–9, Sun 11–2; Sep–Jun Mon, Wed–Sat 11–2, 5–8, Sun 11–2 🖐 Free

a walk from Tamariu

This walk begins with a short stretch of rocky coastline, before heading inland for the gentle climb to the summit of Puig Gruí (154m/505ft).

Start on the beach at Tamariu. From the southern end of the beach, near the car-parking area, cross to the smaller beach of Platja dels Liris and climb the steps, marked with red and white stripes, to join the GR92 coastal path.

Keep to the waymarks. You have to scramble across one rocky cove and climb around the next before levelling out on to a path running behind a stone wall.

At the next cove, climb for a few metres, then turn left through a grove of tamarisk trees. Continue to follow the red and white waymarks.

Eventually the path curves right, following the bend in the sea, then zigzags down to the pebble beach at the tiny cove of Cala Pedrosa.

Take the path directly behind the beach, climbing through the valley; at the top of this path turn right (leaving the GR92) to reach a road. Turn left along this road. After 50m (55yds), take the track on your right, just after a crossroads sign. The path is now marked with yellow and white stripes.

Passing an old well and a vineyard, you climb through a tamarisk wood, with occasional glimpses of the sea to your right, until you reach the summit of Puig Gruí.

Keep to the waymarks. The path turns right and drops steeply through the forest until it reaches a road with a wide circle. Turn right and continue on this road to return to Tamariu.

Distance 8km (5 miles)
Time 2.5 hours
Start/end point Tamariu ✚ 23H 🚌 From Palafrugell in summer
Lunch Es Dofí (➤ 124)

ULLASTRET

Archaeological excavations at Ullastret have revealed most of what we know about the ancient Iberian culture, which thrived here between the 6th and 2nd centuries BC. The Iberians were the first Spanish people to develop a written language; they learned pottery and metallurgy, and established towns and trading centres.

The Iberian settlement at Ullastret is the largest yet discovered in Catalonia. This fortified village was built on what was an island on a marshy lake, but is now at the centre of a fertile plain. Parts of the walls and the defensive towers remain, together with public buildings including cisterns, grain stores and a pair of temples to an unknown god. Most of the remains date from around the 3rd century BC; they were probably built over the foundations of earlier houses. The village was abandoned in the 2nd century BC, and remained deserted until excavations began in 1947.

A museum in the former chapel of Sant Andreu interprets the remains and contains finds from the excavations. There is a model of the site, and the displays describe the Iberian lifestyle (hunting, fishing, quarrying, metalwork), the development of money and of trading with the Greeks, and the rituals of cremation and child burial, which hint at the possibility of child sacrifice.

✚ 21G ✉ Puig de Sant Andreu ☎ 972 17 90 58 🕐 Easter and Jun–Sep Tue–Sun 10–8; Oct–May Tue–Sun 10–2, 3–6 💰 Inexpensive (audio-guide extra)

HOTELS

AIGUABLAVA
Aigua Blava (€€€)
One of the gems of the Catalán coast, with white-painted buildings tumbling down towards a rocky cove. Many rooms are in villas in the gardens; also tennis courts and a pool.

✉ Platja de Fornells ☎ 972 62 20 58; www.aiguablava.com 🕐 Mar–Oct

BEGUR
Rosa (€)
Family-run hotel in the heart of town. Bike hire available.

✉ Carrer Pi i Ralló 11 ☎ 972 62 30 15; www.hotel-rosa.com 🕐 Mar–Nov

BESALÚ
Comte Tallaferro (€€)
Stylish, comfortable rooms in a 16th-century town house. Guests can use the swimming pool at Fonda Siqués, a traditional coaching inn and restaurant run by the same family.

✉ Carrer Ganganell 2 ☎ 972 591609; www.grupcalparent.com 🕐 All year

Maria (€)
Simple rooms around the courtyard of a 16th-century building on central square.

✉ Plaça Llibertat 15 ☎ 972 59 01 06 🕐 All year

LA BISBAL D'EMPORDÀ
Castell d'Empordà (€€€)
Luxury hotel set in a 12th-century castle, with a pool in the extensive gardens and rooms filled with art and antiques.

✉ Castell d'Empordà ☎ 972 646254; www.castelldemporda.com
🕐 Mar–Dec

CALELLA DE PALAFRUGELL
Sant Roc (€€)
Traditional seaside hotel in a spectacular position on a rocky outcrop looking over the bay. Steps lead down to the beach.

✉ Plaça de l'Atlàntic 2 ☎ 972 61 42 50; www.santroc.com 🕐 Apr–Oct

La Torre (€€)

Simple hotel overlooking the bay between Calella and Llafranc.

✉ Passeig de la Torre 28 ☎ 972 61 46 03; www.hotel-latorre.com

🕐 Apr–Sep

GIRONA
Bellmirall (€)

This medieval stone mansion, in the old town, has been turned
into a charming hostel with simple but comfortable rooms
overlooking the cathedral.

✉ Carrer Bellmirall 3 ☎ 972 20 40 09 🕐 Mar–Dec

Ciutat de Girona (€€)

Cool, minimalist design hotel, close to the old town and the river.

✉ Carrer Nord 2 ☎ 972 483038; www.hotel-ciutatdegirona.com

🕐 All year

Peninsula (€€)

Comfortable hotel in an excellent central location, beside the Pont
de Pedra and close to Girona's old town quarter.

✉ Carrer Nou 3 ☎ 972 20 38 00; www.novarahotels.com 🕐 All year

LLAFRANC
El Far (€€€)

Just nine rooms set around an interior courtyard in an old chapel
high on the cliffs. Some of the rooms have magnificent sea views.

✉ Cap de Sant Sebastià ☎ 972 301639; www.elfar.net 🕐 Feb–Dec

Llafranch (€€)

Stylish, comfortable hotel on the seafront promenade, with a
reputation for good food. One of the first tourist hotels on the
Costa Brava, and run by the same family. Salvador Dalí was a
regular visitor; the bar is lined with pictures of him with flamenco
performers and the brothers who ran the hotel.

✉ Passeig de Cípsela 16 ☎ 972 30 02 08; www.hllafranch.com

🕐 All year

PALS
Mas de Torrent (€€€)
An 18th-century farmhouse, with period furniture and flower-filled gardens. Known for its innovative Catalán cuisine.

✉ Torrent, between Pals and Palafrugell ☎ 902 55 03 21; www.mastorrent.com 🕐 All year

PERATALLADA
Cal'Aliu (€)
Simple, attractive rooms in a village house. Breakfast is included and bike rental is available.

✉ Carrer de la Roca 6 ☎ 972 63 40 61 🕐 All year

SANTA PAU
TAMARIU
Tamariu (€€)
A small and friendly hotel right beside the beach.

✉ Passeig del Mar 2 ☎ 972 62 00 31; www.tamariu.com 🕐 Mar–Nov

TORROELLA DE MONTGRÍ
Palau Lo Mirador (€€€)
Luxurious five-star hotel in a converted Gothic palace.

✉ Passeig de l'Església 1 ☎ 972 75 80 63; www.palaulomirador.com 🕐 All year

RESTAURANTS

BEGUR
El Bodegón (€€€)
Fresh local fish is roasted in a wood-burning oven at this back-street restaurant in the old centre of town.

✉ Carrer Pi i Ralló 3 ☎ 972 62 20 13 🕐 Lunch and dinner Tue–Sun

BESALÚ
Ca'n Quei (€)
A good-value bar on a quiet square, serving snacks, sandwiches, salads and hot meals.

✉ Plaça Sant Vicenç ☎ 972 59 00 85 🕐 Lunch and dinner, Thu–Tue

Curia Reial (€€)

This restaurant in the 14th-century Royal Court building specializes in Catalán meat and game dishes. There is a terrace overlooking the river and the medieval bridge.

✉ Plaça Llibertat ☎ 972 59 02 63 ⏱ Lunch and dinner. Closed Tue

Els Fogons de Can Llaudes (€€€)

This elegant restaurant is housed in a Romanesque chapel facing the church of Sant Pere. The emphasis is on meat and game, such as venison, wild boar and roast lamb. Booking essential.

✉ Prat de Sant Pere 6 ☎ 972 59 08 58 ⏱ Lunch and dinner. Closed Tue

CALELLA DE PALAFRUGELL

Can Palet (€€)

Small, attractive seafood restaurant with tables beside the beach.

✉ Carrer Calau 8 ☎ 972 61 45 45 ⏱ Lunch and dinner daily

Tragamar (€€)

Seaside branch of a popular Barcelona restaurant chain, offering designer *tapas* and sophisticated Catalán cuisine in informal, stylish surroundings on the beachside promenade.

✉ Platja del Canadell ☎ 972 61 51 89 ⏱ Lunch and dinner daily. Closed Tue in winter

L'ESTARTIT

La Gaviota (€€€)

Seafood restaurant at the end of the promenade with a good view of the Medes Islands. Among the unusual specialities are red mullet with rosemary, and angler-fish in sea-urchin sauce.

✉ Passeig Marítim 92 ☎ 972 75 20 19 ⏱ Lunch and dinner Tue–Sun

GIRONA

Abril (€)

Fresh, light, healthy salads, meat and fish dishes and a good-value four-course lunchtime menu are served at this pretty little bistro, with tables on the square in summer.

✉ Carrer de Santa Clara 27 ☎ 972 41 10 55 ⏱ Mon–Sat, 8:30–8:30

El Balcó (€€)

This Argentinian restaurant is a paradise for serious meat-lovers, with beef, veal and duck grilled to perfection over an open fire.

✉ Carrer de les Hortes 16 ☎ 972 22 31 61 🕐 Lunch and dinner. Closed Sun

Le Bistrot (€)

Pancakes, salads and crusty bread pizzas at this popular old-style bistro, with tables out of doors on a pretty staircase in summer.

✉ Pujada Sant Domènec 4 ☎ 972 218803 🕐 Lunch and dinner daily

Blanc (€€)

Funky modern design and even funkier food – how about tuna with mango chutney followed by chocolate soup with olive oil?

✉ Carrer Nord 2 ☎ 972 415637 🕐 Lunch and dinner daily

Boira (€€)

Unusual *tapas* downstairs and a smart restaurant upstairs, featuring modern, light versions of traditional Catalán cuisine. Get here early for one of the tables overlooking the river.

✉ Plaça Independència 17 ☎ 972 21 96 05 🕐 Lunch and dinner daily

Café Mozart (€€)

This popular restaurant serves delicious pizzas, cooked in a wood-fired oven, as well as fondues and grilled meat dishes; there is a wide range of salads.

✉ Plaça Independència 2 ☎ 972 20 75 42 🕐 Lunch and dinner. Closed Tue

Casa Marieta (€€)

This popular old standby serves traditional Catalán food, such as seafood casserole and duck with pears, in agreeably old-fashioned surroundings on an arcaded square.

✉ Plaça Independéncia 5 ☎ 972 20 10 16 🕐 Lunch and dinner, Tue–Sun

Creperie Bretonne (€€)

Delicious, authentic French pancakes and cider from Brittany served in offbeat, retro surroundings.

✉ Carrer Cort Reial 14 ☎ 972 21 81 20 🕐 Lunch and dinner, Tue–Sun

Mar Plaça (€€€)

This classy fish restaurant specializes in fish soups and casseroles and also serves delicious simply grilled fresh fish.

✉ Plaça Independència 3 ☎ 972 20 59 62 🕐 Lunch Mon–Sat, dinner Tue–Sat

El Pou del Call (€€)

Come here for good-value Catalán cuisine with an excellent *menú del día*; located in the heart of the Jewish quarter.

✉ Carrer de la Força 14 ☎ 972 22 37 74 🕐 Lunch and dinner. Closed Wed

La Taverna (€)

Tapas, omelettes, local sausages and cheeses, as well as home-made patés and Basque cider, are the favourites here, all served at outdoor tables in the pleasant setting of a new town square.

✉ Plaça Santa Susanna 2 ☎ 972 21 13 81 🕐 Open all day, Mon–Sat

Zanpanzar (€)

A Basque-style *tapas* bar where the *pintxos* (bite-sized open sandwiches) are laid out along the counter. You help yourself and then add up the cocktail sticks on your plate in order to settle your bill. Basque cider is a speciality.

✉ Carrer Cort Reial 12 ☎ 972 21 28 43 🕐 Lunch and dinner, Tue–Sun

OLOT

La Deu (€€)

The famous Garrotxa potato dish *patates de la Deu* was invented at this traditional Catalán restaurant, which offers hearty 'volcanic cooking' in a country house on the edge of town.

✉ Carretera La Deu ☎ 972 26 10 04 🕐 Lunch daily, dinner Mon–Sat

PALAFRUGELL

La Xicra (€€€)

Classic Empordan cooking in a village house. Specials include seafood casserole and chickpeas with baby octopus and ham.

✉ Carrer de Sant Antoni 17 ☎ 972 30 56 30 🕐 Lunch Thu–Tue, dinner Thu–Mon

PALS

Mas de Torrent (€€€)

Innovative meat and fish dishes prepared with typical Catalán flair, in a beautiful 18th-century farmhouse.

✉ Torrent, near Pals ☎ 902 55 03 21 🕐 Lunch and dinner daily

PERATALLADA

Can Bonay (€€)

A third-generation family restaurant offering Catalán classics such as goose with turnips and pig's trotters with snails.

✉ Plaça de les Voltes 13 ☎ 972 63 40 34 🕐 Lunch and dinner, Tue–Sun

La Riera (€€)

Simple Catalán cooking, grilled meat, sausages, snails, at this hotel with a delightful summer terrace on the main square .

✉ Plaça de les Voltes 3 ☎ 972 63 41 42 🕐 Lunch and dinner. Closed Tue in winter

PÚBOL

Can Bosch (€)

Traditional village restaurant serving hearty portions and a good value set lunch.

✉ Beside the castle ☎ 972 48 83 57 🕐 Lunch daily, dinner Fri–Sun

SANT JOAN DE LES ABADESSES

Casa Rudes (€)

Home-cooked Catalán favourites and an old-style grocery shop.

✉ Carrer Major 10 ☎ 972 72 01 15 🕐 Lunch daily, dinner Mon–Sat

SANTA PAU

Cal Sastre (€€)

Garrotxa cuisine featuring local sausages, mushrooms and beans, and located in a delightful square.

✉ Placeta dels Balls 6 ☎ 972 68 04 21 🕐 Lunch Tue–Sun; dinner Tue–Sat

TAMARIU
Es Dofí (€€)
One of the best of the many fish restaurants along the seafront.

✉ Passeig del Mar 22 ☎ 972 62 00 43 🕐 Lunch and dinner daily

SHOPPING

ARTS AND CRAFTS
Avellí
One of the biggest of La Bisbal's pottery shops. If you can't find what you are looking for here, you probably won't find it anywhere.

✉ Carrer l'Aigüeta 60–68, La Bisbal ☎ 972 64 06 02

Bambu Bambu
If you can't face looking at any more pottery, this large shop on La Bisbal's 'ceramic street' has a huge collection of basketware.

✉ Carrer l'Aigüeta 61, La Bisbal ☎ 972 64 23 33

La Bisbal d'Art
Ceramics by local potters Pau Planes and Maria Marquès, produced at their workshop in Corça. The last pottery shop out of town on the road to Girona.

✉ Carrer l'Aigüeta 146, La Bisbal ☎ 972 64 32 32

Bosch
A large pottery emporium selling everyday items like earthenware plates and cooking pots at good prices.

✉ Carrer l'Aigüeta 47, La Bisbal ☎ 972 64 38 19

La Botiga
La Botiga is a pottery and gift shop with a few better pieces hidden away among the displays of tourist kitsch.

✉ Carrer l'Aigüeta 32, La Bisbal ☎ 972 64 18 02

El Càntir
Bright, colourful, locally-made pottery sold at two shops on the main road.

✉ Carrer l'Aigüeta 45 and 126, La Bisbal ☎ 972 64 24 72

Embolic

You can watch the beautiful tapestries being woven at this workshop close to the old town walls.

✉ Avinguda Lluís Companys 22, Torroella de Montgrí ☎ 972 75 85 71

L'Estació

Ming-style vases, homages to the Catalán design gurus such as Miró and Picasso, and ceramic cartoon characters for children can all be found among the casseroles and coffee pots here.

✉ Carrer l'Aigüeta 18, La Bisbal ☎ 972 64 20 97

Fang i Art

All the pottery sold here is guaranteed made by hand in a local workshop. Look for the beautiful Arab-style water-pots.

✉ Carrer l'Aigüeta 76, La Bisbal ☎ 972 64 39 43

Katy

Striking and imaginative pottery in colourful, child-like designs.

✉ Carrer l'Aigüeta 41, La Bisbal ☎ 972 64 38 44

Llensa

The big attraction of Llensa is the wide range of terracotta garden pots, including some antiques in a room at the back.

✉ Carrer l'Aigüeta 91, La Bisbal ☎ 972 64 20 71

Nadal

A retail outlet boasting a big selection of pottery for the kitchen, home and the garden.

✉ Carrer l'Aigüeta 84, La Bisbal ☎ 972 64 03 88

D'Occ Catalonia

Stylish, locally made ceramics and cosmetics are sold at this shop on the main street. There is another branch in Girona, at the entrance to the Jewish quarter at Carrer de la Força 1.

✉ Carrer l'Aigüeta 74, La Bisbal ☎ 972 641462

Pau Planes
Local potters Pau Planes and Maria Marquès produce distinctive modern designs which are on sale in two shops in the village.
✉ Plaça Major 8 and Carrer Major 9, Pals ☎ 972 63 64 02

Plats i Olles
An interesting shop with a good range of locally produced artefacts and gifts, mostly in ceramics and glass.
✉ Carrer Cavallers 33, Palafrugell ☎ 972 30 01 47

Rogenca d'Ullastret
Everything is produced in a local workshop. You can also visit the workshop and exhibition room in the centre of town at Passeig Marimon Asprer 4, on the riverside promenade.
✉ Carrer l'Aigüeta 112, La Bisbal ☎ 972 640482

El Talleret
A range of locally produced pottery which is sold at several shops throughout the town.
✉ Carrer l'Aigüeta 37, 54 and 136, La Bisbal ☎ 972 64 27 08

Vila Clara
This is an arty pottery workshop where everything is designed and made locally and, surprisingly, it is not as expensive as you might expect. There are two shops – one at each end of the town.
✉ Carrer l'Aigüeta 56 and Carrer Sis d'Octubre 27, La Bisbal ☎ 972 64 25 79

Les Voltes
Glass and pottery. Beneath the arches in the square.
✉ Plaça de les Voltes, Peratallada ☎ 972 63 41 21

FOOD AND DRINK
Cacao Sampaka
Rich chocolatey treats including truffles in a variety of unusual flavours.
✉ Carrer Santa Clara 45, Girona ☎ 972 20 23 41

Cal Enric

This factory shop sells a tempting selection of galetes, delicious local biscuits made with butter and almonds. A tasty souvenir to take back home.

✉ Carretera Girona 6, Castellfollit de la Roca ☎ 972 29 40 44

J Candela

This shop sells *turrón* (*torró* in Catalán), produced in the family factory, as well as a range of unusual sweets.

✉ Carrer de l'Argenteria 8, Girona ☎ 972 22 09 38

Museu de l'Embotit

The sausage museum (► 99) sells cured meats from the Sala factory, which has been based here for more than 150 years.

✉ Carretera Girona 10, Castellfollit de la Roca ☎ 972 29 44 63

El Rebost del Comtat

A museum of local history and crafts with a cheese and sausage shop attached, where you can taste before you buy.

✉ Plaça Llibertat 14, Besalú ☎ 972 59 03 07

MARKETS

Mercat Municipal

This indoor market near the Plaça de Catalunya has stalls selling a wide range of meat, fish and cheeses, fresh fruit and vegetables, and ready-prepared meals. A good place to stock up on provisions for a picnic.On Saturdays there arealso outdoor produce markets in the square.

✉ Plaça Salvador Espriu, Girona ⏰ Mon–Sat 7–1:30

Mercat Semanal

Girona's weekly markets take place on Tuesday and Saturday, on the edge of Parc de la Devesa. On Saturdays a flower market is set up on the Rambla, along with arts and crafts stalls on Pont de Pedra.

✉ Passeig de la Devesa, Girona ⏰ Tue, Sat all year

ENTERTAINMENT

BARS AND CLUBS
Excalibur
'Celtic ale house' in the old town; locals and visitors meet to drink British beers.

✉ Plaça de l'Oli 1, Girona ☎ 972 20 82 53

Sala de Ball
Dance hall and nightclub where the locals dance the tango to live orchestras at weekends.

✉ Passeig de la Devesa, Girona ☎ 972 20 14 39

Sunset Jazz Club
Smoky jazz bar with live modern jazz Saturday and Sunday nights.

✉ Carrer Jaume Pons i Martí 12, Girona ☎ 872 08 01 45

MUSIC FESTIVALS
Calella de Palafrugell
A festival of *havaneres* (► 96) is held on the beach on the first weekend in July, and the Costa Brava jazz festival takes place in the gardens of Cap Roig throughout July and August. There are also festivals of *havaneres* in the neighbouring resorts of Llafranc (► 101) and Tamariu (► 112).

☎ 972 30 02 28

Olot
The biggest *sardana* festival in Catalonia (see panel) takes place in Olot on the second Sunday of July, and features up to 5,000 dancers.

☎ 972 26 01 41

Torroella de Montgrí
The international music festival which takes place between July and August is one of the leading musical events in Europe, with performances ranging from chamber music to jazz in the town square and the Gothic church of Sant Genís.

☎ 972 76 10 98

The North Coast and Beyond

This region stretches from the wide Gulf of Roses, with its marshes, estuaries and endless beach, to the wild northern coastline, where the Pyrenees drop into the sea. Foreigners have long been drawn to these shores – it was here that the Greeks and Romans established their first ports – and the area around trendy Cadaqués has become the most fashionable stretch of the Costa Brava.

Figueres
□

The north coast is inextricably linked with Salvador Dalí, whose surreal landscapes owe much to the scenery around Cap de Creus. Take the twisting coast road from Portbou to El Port de la Selva, with the mountains on one side and the sea on the other, then drive across the headland, with its wind-sculpted rocks, and you soon see how the artist and the landscape were made for each other.

FIGUERES

The capital of the Alt
Empordà region would be
just another county town,
were it not for the influence
of its most famous son,
Salvador Dalí. Tourists pour
in by the bus-load to see his
surreal theatre-museum
(▶ 52–53) and Figueres is
enjoying a new-found
prosperity as a result. For
centuries it was an
unassuming market town,
created by royal charter in
1267; now it is firmly
established on the Spanish
tourist circuit.

Long before Dalí's birth
in 1904, Figueres had a
reputation for creativity and
new ideas – federalism,
Republicanism, Modernist
art. The Utopian socialist
Narcís Monturiol, claimed as
the inventor of the
submarine, was born in the
same street as Dalí; it was
another local resident, Pep
Ventura, who created the
modern form of the *sardana*
in the mid-19th century.

✚ 8C

🛈 Plaça del Sol ☎ 972 50 31 55

Barri Antic

Between the Rambla and the Dalí museum lies the centre of old Figueres, now a network of pedestrian shopping streets. Several of these streets converge on Plaça Ajuntament, a peaceful, arcaded square that was once the gateway to the city. The street names leading from the square show Figueres' historical importance as the crossroads of northern Catalonia – Carrer Girona to the south, Carrer Besalú to the west, Carrer La Jonquera to the north and Carrer Peralada to the east.

Restaurants and bars (€–€€)

Castell de Sant Ferran

This star-shaped citadel, begun in 1753 as a defence against the French, was once claimed to be the second-largest fortress in Europe. During the Napoleonic Wars it was captured by French forces, who imprisoned and later executed the hero of the Girona resistance, Alvarez de Castro. From 1904 to 1933 it was a high-security prison, holding some of Spain's most dangerous criminals.

On a one-hour, self-guided audio-tour you can stroll around the castle ramparts and visit the parade ground, chapel and vaulted stables. Even when it is closed you can get a feel for its vast size by walking around the 3km (2-mile) path that encircles the castle walls.

✉ Pujada del Castell ☎ 972 50 60 94 🕔 1 Jul–15 Sep daily 10:30–8; 16 Sep–Jun daily 10:30–3 ✋ Inexpensive ❓ Jeep tours of ramparts, dinghy trips of underground cisterns at weekends and summer; reservations essential

Monestir de Vilabertran

In the village of Vilabertran, 2km (1.2 miles) from Figueres, is an Augustinian abbey which is considered to be one of the finest examples of Catalán Romanesque architecture. The 11th-century basilica, with three aisles, three apses and a tall, square belltower, still stands, together with a 12th-century cloister with plant motifs carved on its capitals. In summer the abbey is the setting for a delightful series of classical music concerts. Among the other buildings are the original chapter house and wine cellar, and a 15th-century Gothic abbots' palace.

✉ On the road from Figueres to Peralada ☎ 972 50 87 87 🕓 Jun–Sep Tue–Sun 10–1, 3–6; Oct–May Tue–Sun 10–1, 3–5 ❓ Classical music festival, Aug–Sep

Museu de l'Empordà

The museum of local art and history was established in 1876 and moved to its present site on the Rambla in 1971. It contains archaeological discoveries from the Iberian, Greek and Roman periods, and a collection of 19th- and 20th-century Catalán art. There are several paintings by Antoni Tàpies, one by Dalí and a lithograph donated by Joan Miró. Artists from Figueres are well represented in the section on Empordan realism. There is also a gallery dedicated to the painters of the Olot School.

✉ Rambla 2 ☎ 972 50 23 05 🕓 Tue–Sat 11–7, Sun 11–2 ✋ Inexpensive (free with entrance ticket for Dalí museum)

Museu del Joguet de Catalunya

In the old Hotel Paris, this toy museum started from one man's collection. Over 3,000 traditional toys are displayed, from cardboard horses to nativity scenes, including a teddy bear that once belonged to Salvador Dalí's sister.

✉ Carrer Sant Pere 1 ☎ 972 50 45 85 ✋ Moderate

Rambla

The heart of Figueres is its Rambla, an attractive tree-lined boulevard built over an old stream with small squares at either end. Whenever he was far from home, Dalí used to reminisce about Figueres' Thursday market, and the pavement cafés on the Rambla on market day are still the best place to get a feel for the pulse of the town. There are two good museums here (▶ opposite), and several Modernist houses, designed by local artist, Josep Azemar.

Nearby, in Plaça Josep Pla, is the Cine-Teatre Jardí, a spectacular *Modernista* theatre, built in 1914.

Teatre-Museu Dalí

Best places to see, pages 52–53.

a walk around Figueres

Start at the station. Cross the small park of Plaça Estació and fork right along Carrer Pompeu Fabra.

Turn right at the end of this street to reach the old grain market, Plaça del Gra, where a market is still held three times a week. Cross this square and take Carrer Concepció to reach Plaça de la Palmera. Turn left towards the Rambla.

A monument to Narcís Monturiol dominates the Rambla's eastern end. Walk down the central avenue, then take Carrer Lasauca, ahead on the left, passing the Hotel Durán, an old Dalí haunt. Cross the ring road at the end of this street to reach the tourist office in Plaça del Sol.

Continue along Carrer Mestre Falla. Take the first right to reach Parc Bosc, a shady and peaceful retreat from the crowds. After exploring the park, return to Passeig Nou and turn left. Cross the main road again and take Carrer Pep Ventura straight ahead.

Emerging on Pujada del Castell, look left for your first glimpse of the Dalí museum. Cross this street into Carrer Besalú. To visit the museum, turn left along Carrer Sant Pere; otherwise, continue straight ahead into the town hall square, Plaça Ajuntament.

Cross this square and take Carrer Peralada to reach the large, ochre-coloured Modernist building, Casino Menestral. Turn right on to Carrer Ample. At the end of the street, look for the plaque opposite, denoting the house on Carrer Monturiol where Salvador Dalí was born. Turn left to return to Plaça de la Palmera and retrace your steps to the station.

Distance 2km (1.2 miles)
Time 1 hour
Start/end point Figueres station 🚇 8C 🚌 To Figueres bus station on Plaça Estació 🚉 Trains from Girona and Portbou
Lunch Durán (➤ 154)

More to see on the North Coast and Beyond

CADAQUÉS
Best places to see, pages 38–39.

CAP DE CREUS
This jagged peninsula, where the Pyrenees jut into the sea, is a place of savage beauty and vicious winds. Salvador Dalí lived just down the road at Portlligat (➤ 142–143), and as you stand on the headland gazing down into secluded creeks it is impossible not to see Daliesque images in the rocks, carved by nature into ever more surreal shapes. This is where the *tramuntana*, the legendary north wind that strikes fear into sailors and fishermen, is at its most violent. If you come when the wind is blowing you will struggle to stay on your feet.

The easiest way to reach the cape is from Cadaqués (➤ 38–39), on a narrow road which snakes across the headland. There is also a coastal footpath from Portlligat, difficult to follow but with the reward of seeing this craggy landscape at its isolated best and dipping into hidden coves along the way. The road ends at a lighthouse, where you can walk on to the slate cliffs and look down over the seascape of deep turquoise water, small islands and rocky coves. This is the easternmost point in mainland Spain and if you come here at dawn you can watch the sun rise over the Iberian peninsula. Sea birds migrate here in winter and wheatears and rock thrushes build their nests in spring, when the cliffs are carpeted with wild flowers and the headland is scented with rosemary and lavender. Swifts and pipits arrive in summer.

🔢 12B 🍴 Restaurant Cap de Creus (➤ 153) 🚌 Cadaqués, 8km (5 miles) away ❓ *Sardana* dancing at sunrise on 1 Jan

ℹ️ Palau de l'Abat, Monestir de Sant Pere de Rodes

Parc Natural de Cap de Creus
☎ 972 19 31 91 🕐 Daily, 10–2, 3–6 ❓ Walking and cycling trails from Sant Pere de Rodes

CASTELLO D'EMPÚRIES

Castelló d'Empúries was the seat of the Counts of Empúries during the Middle Ages and many of its buildings date from then. Its greatest glory is the basilica of Santa Maria, an early Gothic church built on the site of a Romanesque cathedral and considered the second church of Girona province, after Girona Cathedral itself. It is worth visiting just to see the magnificently sculpted portal; inside there is a Romanesque double font and a fine alabaster altarpiece by Vicenç Borràs. Other buildings of note are a 14th-century prison and the El Rentador wash house, with a porticoed atrium, fountain and view of the basilica through its arches.

The nearby resort of Empúria-brava was built in 1967 on the Muga river delta. It consists of a large marina and an extensive network (30km/18.5 miles) of canals, plus hundreds of near-identical whitewashed holiday villas, each with their own private mooring. There is a long beach and facilities for watersports, as well as boat trips on the canals and around the coast. There's also a small aerodrome offering parachuting and pleasure flights. The resort is well laid-out and attractive, but lacks any authentic Catalán feel.

The decision to build Empúria-brava on former marshland led indirectly to the creation of the Aiguamolls de l'Empordà nature reserve (➤ 48–49).

🕂 9C 🍽 A few restaurants and bars in the town (€–€€); many more in Empúria-brava (€–€€€) 🚌 From Cadaqués, Figueres and Girona ❓ Market on Tue; La Verge de Candelera, 2 Feb; Diada del Carme festival at Empúria-brava, 16 Jul; Festa de Sant Llorenç, 10 Aug; Terra dels Trobadors (minstrel festival), 11 Sep.

🛈 Plaça Jaume I ☎ 972 15 62 33

COLERA

This small resort close to the French border has two large pebble beaches set into a horseshoe bay, with a fishing harbour at one end. A flight of steps from the northern beach leads to the Art Parc, where you can clamber over a collection of brightly coloured tile sculptures. Near here is the tiny train station. A road from the station leads to the next bay at Cala Rovellada, with its own small beach.

🕂 10B 🍽 Restaurants and bars in the village and on the harbour (€–€€) 🚉 From Figueres, Girona and Portbou

EMPÚRIES

Best places to see, pages 42–43.

L'ESCALA

What was once just a fishing port has grown into a major holiday resort. There are several good beaches to either side of the town, especially at Cala Montgó to the south. Anchovies have been salted here ever since the Greeks landed at nearby Empúries (▶ 42–43); local sardines are another good buy at the fish auctions which still take place by the harbour each weekday afternoon.

🚌 10E 🍴 Wide choice of restaurants (€–€€€) 🚍 Buses from Figueres, Girona, Palafrugell and Torroella de Montgrí ❓ Market on Sun

LLANÇÀ

Llançà was built 2km (1.2 miles) back from its harbour in an effort to deter pirates, with the result that it is neatly split into two parts. The old town is largely unaffected by tourism; life centres around the Plaça Major, with its outdoor cafés, Romanesque belltower and Baroque parish church. The busy harbour, with beaches to either side, has a pleasant promenade lined with fish restaurants. Climb the rocky outcrop on the edge of the marina for great views of Cap de Creus (➤ 136) poking out to sea.

➕ 10B 🍴 Wide choice of restaurants by the harbour (€€–€€€)
🚌 From Figueres and El Port de la Selva 🚉 Trains from Figueres, Girona and Portbou ❓ Market on Wed

MONESTIR DE SANT PERE DE RODES

Best places to see, pages 46–47.

PARC NATURAL DE L'AIGUAMOLLS

Best places to see, pages 48–49.

PERALADA

The moated Renaissance castle that dominates this village is better known these days as Catalonia's most stylish casino (➤ 156). Entrance to the **castle museum,** with its collections of glass and ceramics and the largest private library in Spain, also gives access to the 14th-century Carmelite convent within the castle walls. Some of the tours also include a tasting of *cava* from the castle cellars. Peralada lies at the centre of the Empordà–Costa Brava wine demarcation and the owners of the castle, the Mateu family, produce some excellent wines.

➕ 8C ❓ International music festival in the castle grounds, Jul–Aug

Museu del Castell

☎ 972 53 81 25 🕐 Guided tours daily from 10am (closed Mon 16 Sep–Jun)
✋ Moderate

EL PORT DE LA SELVA

With its whitewashed houses facing an attractive harbour, this small resort on the edge of the Cap de Creus peninsula looks every bit the timeless Mediterranean fishing village that it almost is. Fishing boats still set out each day to gather the anchovies for which El Port de la Selva is known, but fishing is slowly giving way to tourism. The water is shallow, the beach is long and sandy, and there is good windsurfing in the sheltered bay. The Serra de Roda mountains, with the monastery of Sant Pere de Rodes (► 46–47) looking down, provide the perfect backdrop.

🚩 10B 🍴 Restaurants and bars on the waterfront (€–€€) 🚌 From Cadaqués, Figueres and Llançà 🚢 Excursions to Cap de Creus ❓ Market on Fri

PORTLLIGAT

This small fishing village on the outskirts of Cadaqués (► 38–39), with boats moored on the beach and the gentle waters of the bay enclosed by an offshore island, is where the painter Salvador Dalí made his home. He first moved here with his future wife Gala in 1930 and stayed permanently from 1948 until her death in 1982. His house, **Casa-Museu Dalí,** built over the ruins of a pair of fishermen's cottages, contains typical Daliesque touches – eggs on the roof, camels in the garden and a swimming pool modelled on the Alhambra in Granada. It is now open to the public, largely as

Dalí left it, and a visit here provides a fascinating insight into the artist's troubled mind. Only a few visitors are allowed in at a time, so booking is essential. In summer it is also possible to take a trip on Dalí's old fishing boat, *Gala*, passing isolated coves on the way to Cap de Creus (➤ 136).

➕ 11C 🍴 Chez Pierre (€€) 🚌 Cadaqués

Casa-Museu Dalí

☎ 972 25 10 15 🕐 15 Jun–15 Sep daily 9:30–9; 15 Mar–14 Jun, 16 Sep–6 Jan Tue–Sun 10:30–6 ✋ Expensive ❓ Advance booking is essential. Boat trips daily 10–8 in summer ☎ 617 46 57 57

a drive from Portlligat

This drive takes in all the major sights associated with the life of Salvador Dalí, beginning at his home in Portlligat and ending at his final resting-place in Figueres. It also re-creates the macabre journey made by Dalí's chauffeur, Artur Caminada, on 10 June, 1982, with the body of Dalí's wife, Gala, in the back seat. She had stipulated that she wanted to die in her castle at Púbol and when she died at Portlligat instead it was Caminada's job to carry her 'home'.

Begin by the beach in Portlligat (▶ 142–143) and follow signs to Cadaqués (▶ 38–39). Just before reaching Cadaqués, turn right towards Roses.

Continue on this road as it winds across the cape,
bypassing Roses to head towards Figueres.

When you see Castelló d'Empúries on your right, turn
left at the roundabout towards Sant Pere Pescador
(▶ 146–147).

You now cross the Empordan plain, passing through a
succession of small villages. Turn right in Sant Pere
Pescador to reach Torroella de Fluvià, then turn left on to
the C31. Follow this long straight road, signposted to La
Bisbal, through Verges and Ultramort to Parlavà.

Turn right at the traffic lights in Parlavà. Reaching the
Girona road, turn right again and take the next left to visit
the Castell Gala Dalí, Púbol (▶ 40–41). After visiting the
castle, return to the Girona road.
Before reaching Girona, turn right
on to the N11 towards Figueres.

This road runs parallel to the
motorway towards France with
occasional glimpses of the Pyrenees
to your left. After 30 minutes, take
the exit for Figueres. The Dalí
museum (▶ 52–53) is in the centre
of town.

Distance 115km (71 miles)
Time 2.5 hours plus lunch and visit to
Castell Gala Dalí, Púbol
Start point Portlligat ✚ 11C
End point Figueres ✚ 8C
Lunch Can Bosch (€) ✉ Púbol
☎ 972 48 83 57

PORTBOU

'Benvinguts' ('Welcome'), says a sign in Catalán at the entrance to this town, leaving day-trippers from France in no doubt that they have arrived in Catalonia, as well as Spain. The opening of the international railway station in 1878 transformed this fishing village into a busy transport hub and there is now a road across the border as well, to the French port of Cerbère. High-speed trains from Paris to Barcelona will eventually pass through Portbou. At the centre of town, the Rambla de Catalunya is an attractive tree-lined boulevard and there is another pretty promenade in front of the pebble beach.

➕ 10A 🍴 Restaurants on waterfront (€€) 🚊 Trains from Figueres and Girona

ROSES

Best places to see, pages 50–51.

SANT PERE PESCADOR

The village of 'St Peter the Fisherman' was built 3km (2 miles) back from the sea to provide a safe haven from pirates, with the unforeseen result that

THE NORTH COAST AND BEYOND

it has largely escaped the Costa Brava's tourist boom. While other fishing ports have been transformed into mass-market, modern resorts, Sant Pere Pescador remains a peaceful, workaday place, where farmers and fruit-growers mingle with occasional foreign tourists on the banks of the River Fluvià.

There is a 17th-century baroque church and the remains of an old castle, but the real attraction of Sant Pere Pescador is its beach, a long and lonely stretch of sand on the shores of the Gulf of Roses. There are no high-rise hotels here, just campsites among the dunes; come out of season when the campsites are closed and you can have sweeping views of the bay all to yourself.

The coastline is protected from development by being part of the Aiguamolls de l'Empordà natural park (➤ 48–49). The protected area also includes the banks of the Fluvià, on both sides of the village. You can walk along well-marked paths to reach the Illa de Caramany, a wooded island and bird reserve created when the course of the river was diverted in 1979.

Close to Sant Pere Pescador are a number of interesting medieval villages, rising above the flat Empordan plain. Sant Miquel de Fluvià is best known for its 11th-century Romanesque abbey, while Sant Tomàs de Fluvià also has an 11th-century priory church, with recently discovered murals.

✚ 9D 🍴 Restaurants and bars (€–€€) 🚌 From L'Escala, Figueres and Palafrugell

SERRA DE L'ALBERA

The Albera mountain range, on the French border, is where the
Pyrenees begin their long descent into the sea. It is a place of
frontier villages and mountain passes, of vineyards, olive groves
and cork forests and, in the north, a natural park which offers
excellent walking along tracks once used by smugglers and
refugees.

The park's information centre is at Espolla, a village of narrow
streets huddled around a church. Espolla is at the heart of the
Costa Brava's wine industry, and at co-operatives outside the

village you can taste and buy the local *Vi de l'Empordà*. The area around Espolla is also known to archaeologists as the place with the greatest concentration of megalithic monuments in Catalonia, with tombs, rock carvings and standing stones dating back to 3500BC. One of the easiest to reach is the Dolmen de la Cabana Arqueta, a burial chamber between Espolla and the next village of Sant Climent de Sescebes. Other paths from Espolla lead to the Dolmen del Barranc, with human and animal figures carved into the roof, and to the standing stones at Rabós d'Empordà, from where a mountain track leads to the 11th-century monastery of Sant Quirze de Colera.

A hair-raising drive from Sant Climent, best attempted in an off-road vehicle, snakes across the mountains to the Castell de Requesens, a restored medieval castle on the site of an earlier fortress. A good road from here, through the village of Cantallops, leads to the border crossing at La Jonquera, where lorries thunder past on the motorway from Paris to Barcelona.

🕂 8A 🍴 Restaurants in Espolla, Garriguella and Sant Climent (€–€€)
🚌 Bus from Figueres to Espolla

Parc Natural de Serra de l'Albera

ℹ️ Carrer del Mossèn Amadeu Sudrià 3, Espolla ☎ 972 54 50 79

HOTELS

CADAQUÉS

Llané Petit (€€)

Beachside hotel on the southern side of the bay, a short walk from the town centre. On the way into town you pass Port Alguer, a scene from a Dalí painting which has hardly changed since he captured it in 1924.

✉ Carrer Dr Bartomeus 37 ☎ 972 25 10 20; www.llanepetit.com
🕑 Mar–Dec

Playa Sol (€€)

Old-fashioned seaside hotel with a swimming pool in the gardens and a small beach decked out with fishing boats directly opposite.

✉ Platja Pianc 3 ☎ 972 25 81 00; www.playasol.com 🕑 Mar–Oct

Rocamar (€€)

Traditional seaside hotel with a sea water pool and steps down to a rocky cove.

✉ Carrer Dr Bartomeus ☎ 972 25 81 50; www.rocamar.com 🕑 All year

CASTELLÓ D'EMPÚRIES

Canet (€€)

Delightful town-centre hotel with a swimming pool in its interior courtyard.

✉ Plaça Joc de la Pilota 2 ☎ 972 25 03 40; www.hotelcanet.com
🕑 Mar–Oct

Hotel de la Moneda (€€)

Four-star hotel in a restored 17th-century mansion in the old Jewish quarter. Facilities include a pool and free internet access.

✉ Plaça de la Moneda 8 ☎ 972 15 86 02; www.hoteldelamoneda.com
🕑 Mar–Nov

Palau Macelli (€€)

Stay in a restored 17th-century Italian palace near the cathedral. Carriage rides available; dinner is served in the garden in summer.

✉ Carrer Carbonar 1 ☎ 972 250567; www.palaumacelli.com 🕑 All year

EMPÚRIES
Hostal Empuriés (€€)
Newly refurbished, old-style beach hotel, near the Greek and Roman ruins.

✉ Platja de Portitxol ☎ 972 77 02 07; www.hostalempuries.com 🕐 All year

FIGUERES
Durán (€€)
An atmospheric, old-world hotel in the centre of town, where Salvador Dalí used to meet his friends for lunch. It also has one of the finest restaurants in Figueres.

✉ Carrer Lasauca 5 ☎ 972 50 12 50; www.hotelduran.com 🕐 All year

Empordà (€€)
This stylish hotel was the birthplace of the new Catalán cuisine and is still an essential place of pilgrimage for food-lovers.

✉ Antiga Carretera de França (N11) ☎ 972 50 05 62; www.hotelemporda.com 🕐 All year

PERALADA
Golf Peralada (€€€)
Five-star golf and spa resort located at the centre of the golf course. Among the facilities is a vinotherapy wine spa.

✉ Carrer Rocabertí ☎ 972 538830; www.golfperalada.com 🕐 All year

EL PORT DE LA SELVA
Porto Cristo (€€)
A comfortable three-star hotel, set just back from the beach in a restored 19th-century house.

✉ Carrer Major 69 ☎ 972 38 70 62; www.hotelportocristo.com 🕐 Feb–Nov

PORTLLIGAT
Calina (€€)
This apartment-style hotel, close to the beach, has a series of self-catering apartments set around a swimming pool.

✉ Portlligat ☎ 972 25 88 51; www.hotelcalina.com 🕐 Mar–Oct

Portlligat (€€)

A peaceful, two-star hotel with a swimming pool and views over Dalí's house and out to sea.

✉ Portlligat ☎ 972 25 81 62 🕐 All year

ROSES

Almadraba Park (€€€)

Four-star hotel with modern facilities, on a rocky cliff overlooking the cove of Almadrava.

✉ Platja de Almadrava ☎ 972 25 65 50; www.almadrabapark.com
🕐 Apr–Oct

Canyelles Platja (€€)

A typical seaside hotel with a swimming pool and facing the Canyelles beach, to the southeast of the town.

✉ Platja Canyelles ☎ 972 25 65 00; www.hotelcanyelles.com 🕐 Apr–Sep

Vistabella (€€€)

This five-star hotel, beside the beach at Canyelles, has its own landing-stage for boats and offers spa-like treatments, ranging from massage to Turkish baths.

✉ Cala Canyelles Petites ☎ 972 25 62 00; www.vistabellahotel.com
🕐 May–Sep

RESTAURANTS

CADAQUÉS

Casa Anita (€€)

At Casa Anita the simple, rustic home cooking is served at communal wooden tables. The authentic atmosphere is a popular choice for locals and tourists alike.

✉ Carrer Miquel Rosset 16 ☎ 972 25 84 71 🕐 Lunch and dinner, Tue–Sun

La Sirena (€€)

Fresh fish and vegetarian choices in this intimate restaurant, hidden away in the back streets of the Jewish quarter around the church.

✉ Carrer d'es Call ☎ 972 25 89 74 🕐 Lunch and dinner, Wed–Sun

CAP DE CREUS
Cap de Creus (€€)

This English-run bar beside the lighthouse offers curries, salads, *tapas* and fresh fish dishes. The panoramic terrace is great for a sunset drink.

✉ Cap de Creus ☎ 972 19 90 05 🕐 Daily 10am–1am in summer, Mon–Thu 12–8, Fri–Sun 11–11 in winter

EMPÚRIES
Mesón del Conde (€€)

The best of the restaurants in the village of Sant Martí d'Empúries is just a short walk from the ruins. In spring try grilled *calçots*, a local onion served with *romesco* sauce.

✉ Plaça Major, Sant Martí d'Empúries ☎ 972 77 03 06 🕐 Lunch and dinner daily in summer, closed Mon eve and Tue in winter

L'ESCALA
Els Pescadors (€€€)

Traditional Catalán cooking using top-quality local ingredients – grilled fish, fresh seafood and *sarsuela* fish casserole.

✉ Carrer Port d'en Perris 3 ☎ 972 77 07 28 🕐 Lunch and dinner daily. Closed Nov and Sun eve in winter

FIGUERES
Antaviana (€€)

Stylish Catalán and French cuisine with an emphasis on duck – try the *carpaccio* of duck breast or the beef in Cabrales (blue cheese) sauce.

✉ Carrer Llers 5 ☎ 972 51 03 77 🕐 Lunch and dinner Wed–Sun

Dalícatessen (€)

This trendy sandwich and salad bar is a good place for a snack before or after a visit to the Dalí museum.

✉ Carrer Sant Pere 19 ☎ 972 51 11 93 🕐 Daily 8am–9pm

Durán (€€)

Salvador Dalí's favourite hangout is still full of character, and continues to serve good local food in a traditional Catalán style.

✉ Carrer Lasauca 5 ☎ 972 50 12 50 🕔 Lunch and dinner daily

Empordà (€€€)

This famous hotel, just outside Figueres on the old road to France, has a magnificent garden terrace, where traditional Empordan cooking is served up with modern flair. The former chef here, Josep Mercader, is considered to be the founder of modern Catalán cuisine.

✉ Antiga Carretera de França ☎ 972 50 05 62 🕔 Lunch and dinner daily

El Setrill d'Or (€)

For good pizzas, fresh pasta dishes and an excellent-value set lunch, with comfortable furnishings and oil paintings on the walls.

✉ Carrer Tortellà 12 ☎ 972 50 55 40 🕔 Lunch and dinner, Wed–Sun

LLANÇÀ
La Brasa (€€)

Local squid and anchovies, seafood casserole and charcoal-grilled meat, served on a pretty terrace just back from the harbour.

✉ Plaça Catalunya 6 ☎ 972 38 02 02 🕔 Lunch and dinner daily, Jul–Aug. Closed Mon eve and Tue Sep–Jun

PERALADA
Mas Moli (€€€)

Roast lamb and suckling pig, cooked in an old-style wood oven, and housed in the setting of an old mill.

✉ Carretera Antiga de Vilabertran ☎ 972 53 82 81 🕔 Lunch Tue–Sun, dinner Tue–Sat

PORTLLIGAT
Chez Pierre (€€)

Intimate, stylish bistro offering French and Catalán cuisine with a hint of oriental influence.

✉ Carrer Miquel Rosset 48 ☎ 972 25 84 16 🕔 Dinner only, Wed–Mon

ROSES
El Bulli (€€€)
Quite simply one of the finest restaurants in Spain. Book ahead.
✉ Cala Montjoi ☎ 972 15 04 57 🕐 Dinner only, Apr–Jun, Wed–Sun;
Jul–Sep daily

Flor de Lis (€€€)
Sophisticated French and seafood cuisine in a pretty cottage in
the back streets.
✉ Carrer Coscanilles 47 ☎ 972 25 43 16 🕐 Dinner only, Wed–Mon,
Easter–Oct

La Llar (€€€)
Creative Catalán cuisine in a delightfully restored farmhouse just
outside the town. The adventurous can try the 'surprise menu'.
✉ Carretera Figueres km4 ☎ 972 25 53 68 🕐 Lunch and dinner daily.
Closed Wed eve and Thu in winter

SERRA DE L'ALBERA
Moli de Vent (€€)
Grilled meat and seasonal game in a rustic old windmill with
stuffed boars' heads on the walls.
✉ Carretera de Roses, Garriguella ☎ 972 53 00 98 🕐 Varies according
to season

SHOPPING

MARKETS
Cadaqués – Mon; Castelló d'Empúries – Tue; L'Escala – Sun;
Figueres – Tue, Thu, Sat; Llançà – Wed; El Port de la Selva – Fri;
Roses – Sun

WINE
La Botiga del Celler
Wines from the castle cellars, including some fine cavas or
sparkling wines.
✉ Plaça del Carme 1, Peralada ☎ 972 53 80 11

ENTERTAINMENT

CASINO
Casino Castell de Peralada
Tapestries line the walls of this moated Renaissance castle where you can play roulette, blackjack or *boule* in an atmosphere of elegance, luxury and fine dining.

✉ Castell de Peralada ☎ 972 53 81 25 🕒 Mon–Thu 8pm–4am, Fri–Sat 7pm–5am, Sun 7pm–4am

CLUB
L'Hostal
Jazz club where Salvador Dalí spent an evening with Mick Jagger and Gabriel García Márquez, and still the in place to meet.

✉ Passeig del Mar 8, Cadaqués ☎ 972 25 80 00 🕒 Daily 5pm–5am

MUSIC FESTIVALS
Cadaqués
An international festival of arts and music, both classical and contemporary, takes over this artists' village in August each summer.

☎ 972 25 83 15

Castelló d'Empúries
Music festival in the cathedral in August and a festival of minstrels, with traditional Catalán songs, on 11 September.

☎ 972 15 62 33

Figueres
A music festival takes place each August and September in the old monastery and church of Vilabertran.

☎ 972 50 01 17

Peralada
Top international performers appear each July and August in evening concerts in the grounds of the castle.

☎ 972 53 82 92

The South and Beyond

Anyone who visited the Costa Brava in 1950 would not recognise this region today. Huge concrete resorts have been created out of little more than fishing harbours, and in summer the coastline reverberates to the sound of the disco beat. Resorts like Lloret de Mar and Platja d'Aro led the way into mass tourism and they are still among the busiest in Spain.

□ Vic

□ Mataró

Not everywhere on the south coast is like this. Sant Feliu de Guíxols and Tossa de Mar are also popular resorts, but their old towns retain a lot of charm. Towns like Blanes and Palamós are still fishing ports as well as tourist centres. And even on the most crowded stretches of coastline it is still possible to find a hidden cove, a reminder of what the Costa Brava used to be before the tourists took over.

BLANES

The Costa Brava starts at Sa Palomera, a rocky promontory halfway along the beach, and continues north all the way to France. Once used for shelter by the town's fishing fleet, the promontory has the remains of an old fire-tower – a primitive lighthouse – at its summit and it is still lit up by fire each year during the Costa Brava's international fireworks contest in July.

Climb on to Sa Palomera, passing the fishing boats which are washed up on the shingle beach, for some of the best views of Blanes. South of here, the beach stretches on, as far as the eye can see, passing hotels, campsites and the mouth of the River Tordera at the start of the Costa Maresme (➤ 161). To the north, a wide promenade with gardens, play areas and restaurant tables on the street leads around to the town's attractive, and still busy, fishing harbour.

Blanes is still a working fishing port, where the arrival of the fleet each evening is followed by an animated auction in the fish market – you can watch it all happening from the upstairs bar. Fishermen mend their nets, old men sit on the sea walls and the sailors' chapel of Nostra Senyora de l'Esperança is adorned with nautical themes. Blanes may be one of the Costa Brava's largest

resorts, but with a population of more than 20,000 it has managed to absorb the tourists without losing its soul.

The old town, just behind the seafront, has survived almost unscathed, with Gothic churches, medieval houses, fountains, shrines and a lively daily produce market. Out of season this is a real Catalán town, best experienced during the sunset promenade when everyone from grandmothers to tiny children put on their best clothes and stroll beside the sea.

Just above the town is the **Mar i Murtra** botanic garden, dramatically situated on a clifftop. There is a splendid collection of South American cactus plants, plus Californian and Chilean palms, spiny aloe from South Africa and a charming Mediterranean garden with olive, pine and tamarisk trees dropping down towards the sea. From the Linnaeus rotunda you can look down over a small cove of sparkling turquoise water and cliffs where the bushes grow wild out of the rocks. This is a very special and peaceful place, even for those who have little interest in plants. You can walk around the guided trail in less than an hour, but you could easily spend a day here, with a good book and a picnic, enjoying the sun and the shade and the sound of the sea.

The road beyond the gardens continues to the small beach and former tuna-fishing port at Cala Sant Francesc, where there is a beach bar in summer. You can also walk or drive from the gardens to the Castell de Sant Joan, an 11th-century castle and 15th-century hermitage with sweeping views of the town's beach.

✚ 19M 🍴 Restaurants (€–€€€) 🚍 From Girona and Lloret de Mar
🚌 From Figueres and Girona 🛥 To other south coast resorts in summer
🛈 Passeig de Catalunya 2 ☎ 972 33 03 48

Mar i Murtra

✉ Passeig Karl Faust 9 ☎ 972 33 08 26 🕐 Jun–Sep daily 9–8; Apr–May, Oct daily 9–6; Nov–Mar daily 10–5 ✋ Moderate 🚍 From Plaça de Catalunya

CALDES DE MALAVELLA

This market town, 15km (9 miles) south of Girona, has been famous for its hot springs since Roman times: recent excavations uncovered the remains of two Roman spas. The town enjoyed a revival during the mid-19th century, when it took advantage of the European fashion for 'taking the waters'. Dr Modest Furest marketed its bottled water under the name Vichy Catalán – a name seen on mineral water bottles throughout Spain to this day. People still come to Caldes to take the waters at the two spa hotels, built around the turn of the 20th century in neo-classical and Modernist style. They offer a range of health and beauty treatments and are particularly recommended for those with digestive and respiratory disorders.

Caldes is at the centre of the wooded Selva landscape and would make a good base for a healthy walking, cycling or horse-riding holiday.

🚩 19J 🍽 Restaurants and bars (€–€€) 🚌 Buses from Girona and Palafrugell 🚆 Trains from Figueres and Girona ❓ Market on Tue

CALONGE

The old village of Calonge is split into two parts: the medieval centre, 2km (1.2 miles) from the sea, dominated by its Gothic castle; and the modern tourist resort of Sant Antoni de Calonge, with hotels, villas and campsites strung out along the coast road between Palamós and Platja d'Aro. From the village there are some pleasant drives through forests of cork and holm oak – north to La Bisbal (➤ 95), or west to Romanyà de la Selva, where a 4,000-year-old burial chamber stands in a lonely spot in the woods, surrounded by a stone circle.

➕ 22J 🍴 Restaurants and bars in Sant Antoni de Calonge (€–€€) 🚌 Buses from Girona, Palafrugell and Palamós ❓ Markets: Calonge, Thu; Sant Antoni de Calonge, Wed

COSTA MARESME

This stretch of 'marshy coast', which runs south from Blanes, is very different in character from the Costa Brava. Nobody would call it rugged – this is a narrow, flat coastal strip, where the beaches are mostly artificial and the villages are cut off from the sea by a busy highway and railway line. The resorts here are mainly used by weekend visitors from Barcelona in search of a change of scenery, though the area's popularity with German tourists has also earned it the nickname *Costa dels Alemanys*. Behind the coast the countryside is known as Catalonia's market garden, where fruit and vegetables and the region's famous carnations are grown.

The coastal highway begins just south of Blanes, near the town of Malgrat de Mar. Next comes Pineda de Mar, where the remains of a Roman aqueduct can be seen. The road continues through a succession of old fishing villages, now almost completely given over to tourism. Sant Pol de Mar is an attractive village with a marina, sandy beaches and a 12th-century hilltop monastery, while Canet de Mar is known for its Modernist architecture. Arenys de Mar, an hour out of Barcelona, is still a working fishing port, with a daily fish market by the harbour, a long tradition of white bobbin-lace-making and a shady Rambla leading up to the town. Near here is Caldes d'Estrac, a spa town since Roman times. Finally you reach Mataró, the capital of the region; beyond here are the suburbs of Barcelona. South of Mataró, at Vilassar de Mar, is the flower market where the florists along Barcelona's Ramblas come to buy their wares.

➕ 19M 🚉 From Blanes to most of the resorts 🚢 From Blanes to Calella de la Costa in summer ❓ Markets: Arenys de Mar, Sat; Caldes d'Estrac, Fri; Calella de la Costa, Sat; Canet de Mar, Wed; Malgrat de Mar, Thu; Pineda de Mar, Fri; flower market at Vilassar de Mar, Mon, Wed, Fri 9–1, 3–5

LLORET DE MAR

Fifty years ago Lloret de Mar was still a fishing village; now it has been transformed into a pulsating resort whose population rises to 200,000 in summer and where it is easier to get a hamburger than a Spanish meal. The main thoroughfare, Carrer la Riera, is a non-

stop strip of discos, bars and amusement arcades, busy day and night. Since the 1990s there have been attempts to change Lloret's image, but that seems to be missing the point. If you want fun in the sun, there's no better place.

The main attraction is the beach. The best sheltered swimming is at the north end, beneath the mock castle on the smaller beach of Sa Caleta. Several more beaches are within easy reach – Cala Gran and Cala Canyelles to the north, Platja de Fenals and Santa Cristina to the south. This last is the setting for a traditional festival each July, when the people of Lloret make a pilgrimage by boat, carrying a statue of their patron saint to the hermitage bearing her name. The old town lies just behind the promenade. Look for the 16th-century parish church, with its unusual *Modernista* tiled roof.

✚ 19L 🍴 Wide choice of restaurants and bars (€–€€€) 🚌 From Blanes, Girona and Tossa de Mar 🚢 To other south coast resorts in summer
❓ Market on Tue; Festa de Santa Cristina, 24–26 Jul

a drive along the coast from Lloret de Mar

This drive takes in the most dramatic stretch of coast road in the Costa Brava.

Start at the car park at the north end of the beach, beside the sardana statue. Take the road that leads uphill, away from the sea, and turn right at the traffic lights towards Tossa de Mar.

Once you leave Lloret the road begins to climb, and there are various *miradors* where you can pull over and admire the sea views. After passing through Tossa de Mar (► 54–55) the road twists and turns through a dizzying series of bends, with cork woods to your left and cliffs dropping into the sea on your right.

Follow this coast road for 20km (12.5 miles), then turn right into Sant Feliu de Guíxols (► 168–169). Turn left along the seafront and left again at the end of the beach, following signs to Platja d'Aro. Pass through the centre of this resort (► 166–167) and continue to Sant Antoni de Calonge, where you turn left towards Calonge (► 160–161).

From Calonge a minor road winds its way through the forest to the pottery town of La Bisbal (► 95).

Reaching La Bisbal, turn right towards Palafrugell. Keep on this road as it bypasses Palafrugell and continues south towards Palamós (► 166).

Keep going south on the coast road from Palamós, retracing your route from Sant Antoni de Calonge. The views along the corniche from Sant Feliu to Tossa are completely different when seen from the other direction.

Distance 130km (80 miles)
Time 4 hours
Start/end point Lloret de Mar ✚ 19L
Lunch Bahía (€€) ✉ Passeig del Mar 17, Sant Feliu de Guíxols ☎ 972 32 02 19

PALAMÓS

This fishing port at the eastern end of
Palamós bay was founded in 1277 and
soon became an important naval base:
when the Aragonese fleet conquered
Sicily in 1299, it sailed from Palamós.
In the 19th century Palamós was the
chief export harbour for Catalonia's
cork industry, and despite the growth
of tourism the town retains a
significant commercial base today. The
fishing fleet still sails each day from
Palamós and its arrival each afternoon
is followed by a lively fish auction by
the harbour.

The old quarter, dominated by the
Gothic church of Santa Maria, stands
on a headland overlooking the harbour.
Several shops here specialize in cork
artefacts from the continuing small-
scale cork industry. A former
warehouse on the dockside houses
the Museu de la Pesca (Fishing Museum), with exhibits exploring
the town's seafaring traditions. The museum offers boat trips
around the bay on an old lateen sailing vessel, *Rafael*, built in 1915.
✚ 22J 🍴 Restaurants (€–€€€) 🚌 From Girona, Palafrugell and Platja d'Aro
🛥 To other south coast resorts in summer ❓ Market on Tue; carnival, week
before Lent; Mare de Déu del Carme, procession of fishing boats on 16 Jul

PLATJA D'ARO

The small fishing harbour of the village of Castell d'Aro has grown
over the last 50 years into the Costa Brava's second largest resort,
with a population that rises from 3,000 in winter to more than
100,000 in summer. The beach is 3km (2 miles) of golden sand; the

nightlife is legendary and there are numerous activities for children. From discos to watersports, whatever you want in Platja d'Aro is probably there – except peace and quiet.

The original village survives 3km (2 miles) inland, with a medieval castle where art exhibitions are sometimes held, and a Museu de la Nina (Doll Museum). For those who want to escape from the beach, there are free guided walking tours of the old village throughout the year.

➕ 22J 🍽 Wide choice of restaurants (€–€€€) 🚌 From Girona, Palamós and Palafrugell ⛴ To other south coast resorts in summer ❓ Market on Fri; carnival, week before Lent

ℹ Carrer Verdaguer 4 ☎ 972 81 71 79

S'AGARÓ

This exclusive villa development, on a headland between the beaches of Sant Pol and Sa Conca, was begun around 1924, when industrialist Josep Ensesa commissioned architect Rafael Masó to design the first houses. Built in his classical *noucentista* style, the resort is an attractive mix of Italianate villas, landscaped gardens and a coastal promenade around a succession of rocky coves. Masó's work was completed in the 1940s by Francesc Folguera, who designed the neo-baroque church at the centre of the resort. Film stars and politicians have long flocked to S'Agaró's famous hotel, Hostal de la Gavina, designed by Masó as a Gothic villa and given a more austere classical style by Folguera. Like the rest of the resort, the hotel is elegant and attractive, but has an air of exclusivity which can be off-putting.

➕ 21K 🍽 Beachside restaurants at Platja Sant Pol (€€); Hostal de la Gavina (€€€)

SANT FELIU DE GUÍXOLS

This used to be the Costa Brava's busiest resort. It's a handsome and dignified town, where most of the building took place before the 1960s high-rise boom. Fishing and boat-building are important industries, and during the 19th century the town grew rich on the export trade in cork. The elegant Modernist buildings on the seafront are a reminder of this wealth: look out for Casino la Constancia, a Moorish-style edifice with arches, mosaics and turrets and an old-style café on the ground floor.

Sant Feliu grew up around its Benedictine monastery, of which all that remains is the Porta Ferrada, a pre-Romanesque atrium with horseshoe arches. The same complex of buildings includes the parish church, built over the monastery ruins, and a small **Museu d'Història** (history museum) containing local artefacts and archaeological finds.

The main beach is a wide arc of sand with a fishing harbour at its north end. From the beachfront promenade, Rambla Vidal with its toy museum leads into the old town of narrow streets and squares. The market square contains an unusual 1929 market hall, with art deco touches and bright stained glass. From the southern end of the beach, a road climbs 2km (1.2 miles) to the chapel of Sant Elm. A tourist 'train' runs up here regularly in summer.

✠ 21K 🍴 Restaurants (€–€€€) 🚌 From Girona, Palafrugell and Palamós 🚢 To other south coast resorts in summer ❓ Market on Sun; carnival procession, Sun before Lent; Mare de Déu del Carme, procession of fishing boats on 16 Jul

ℹ️ Plaça del Mercat ☎ 972 82 00 51

Museu d'Història

✉ Plaça del Monestir ☎ 972 82 15 75 🕐 Tue–Sat 10–1, 5–8, Sun 10–1 ✋ Free

SERRA DE MONTSENY

The Montseny mountain range is an attractive region of cork, pine and beech forests, villages and mountain streams, straddling the border between Girona and Barcelona provinces, just inland from the southern Costa Brava. It's well known for its springs: much of the country's mineral water is bottled here, especially in the spa town of Sant Hilari Sacalm.

There are two routes into the Serra de Montseny from the coast. Both involve heading for the A7 motorway, which you can leave at the junctions for either Hostalric or Sant Celoni. A circuit of the region, beginning at Hostalric and returning via Sant Celoni, would make a good full-day excursion from one of the south coast resorts.

Hostalric is a medieval walled village, perched on a basalt rock and surrounded by cork forests; a short drive west leads to Breda, known for its pottery shops. The road continues north to Arbúcies, where there is a museum of local crafts in the porticoed town square, before snaking through the mountains to the charming village of Viladrau. From here there is a choice of routes south to Sant Celoni – one via Seva, through the village of Montseny itself, the other passing the region's highest peak, Turó de l'Home (1,706m/5,597ft). At the hermitage of Santa Fé, beneath Turó de l'Home, there is an information centre and a choice of several waymarked walks. Here you are at the heart of the Serra de Montseny nature reserve, and you may see peregrines, eagle owls and red squirrels.

➕ 14L 🍴 Restaurants in all the towns and villages (€–€€€) 🚌 From Girona to Sant Hilari Sacalm ❓ Markets in Arbúcies, Breda and Sant Hilari Sacalm, Sun; Living Via Crucis, re-enactment of Christ's crucifixion on Good Friday, Sant Hilari Sacalm; Enramades, ancient festival of floral art on the Sun after Corpus Christi, Arbúcies; Festa del Flabiol, flute festival in Arbúcies, late Oct

Parc Natural de Serra de Montseny
ℹ️ Fontmartina, Santa Fé ☎ 938 47 51 02

TOSSA DE MAR
Best places to see, pages 54–55.

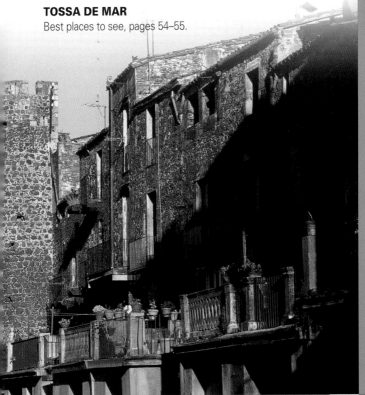

VIC

The opening of the C25 highway, tunnelling through the north of the Montseny mountain range from Girona, has brought the ancient market town of Vic within easy reach of the coast. This is a town known even among Catalans as the essence of Catalonia, with an attractive medieval centre containing architecture from Roman to Modernist, enclosed by a ring road on the site of the old city walls.

The best time to visit Vic is on a market day (Tuesday or Saturday), when the main square, Plaça Major, is buzzing with life. Fruit and vegetables are sold at one end, flowers at the other, while the arcades around the edges shelter everything from baby chicks to second-hand books. Stalls at the centre of the square sell bric-à-brac, pottery, household utensils and cheap clothes, and a crafts and wholefood market is set up in the neighbouring square, Plaça del Pes. The butchers and sausage-makers on Carrer dels

Argenters do a brisk business (Vic has long been renowned for its *fuet* and *botifarra* sausages) and the streets of the old town echo with gossip. By 3pm the bars are full and the market has been cleared away; by 4pm the cleaners have done their job, the cafés have put out their chairs and you can sit in the sun and appreciate Plaça Major as it is the rest of the week, with pigeons in the square, children playing in the sand and no sign that a market has taken place at all.

✚ 13J

Catedral

Vic's cathedral was begun in the 11th century, but the present building dates from 1803, when the Romanesque belltower was incorporated into a new neo-classical design. Parts of the original cloister survive, with a 14th-century Gothic cloister on top. The most unusual

feature is the set of wall paintings by the Catalán mural artist Josep Maria Sert. His first paintings were damaged by fire during the Spanish Civil War and the replacements were inaugurated only days before his death in 1945. The striking red and gold colours and apocalyptic Biblical scenes form a powerful link between the persecution suffered by Christ and that felt by Catalonia at the hands of Spain. Sert is buried in the cloisters. A few of the remaining pieces from his first decoration of the cathedral are displayed in the Capella de la Pietat, a baroque chapel on Carrer Cardona.

✉ Plaça de la Catedral ☎ 938 86 44 49 🕐 Daily 10–1, 4–7 🖑 Free (cloister and crypt inexpensive)

Museu de l'Art de la Pell

Tanning is one of Vic's traditional industries, and the Leather
Museum, housed in a former convent, contains an unusual
collection of leather artefacts from around the world. There are
chopstick holders from China, funerary face masks from
Cameroon, embossed armchairs from Portugal, suitcases from
Peru, shadow puppets from Thailand, religious paintings from
Spain and a riding saddle from Mexico, all collected by Andreu
Colomer i Munmany.

✉ Carrer Arquebisbe Alemany 5 ☎ 938 83 32 79 🕐 Tue–Sat 11–2, 5–8,
Sun 11–2 🎟 Free

Museu Episcopal

The diocesan museum contains more than 20,000 exhibits,
including the most complete collection of Catalán Romanesque
art outside Barcelona. The treasures on display include frescoes
and altarpieces from remote Pyrenean churches, and some

wonderfully lifelike 12th-century wooden statues of the Virgin. Also here are Gothic religious paintings by some of Catalonia's finest artists, including Lluís Borrassa, Bernat Martorell and Jaume Huguet. The museum is housed in a magnificent new building which opened next to the cathedral in 2002.

🗷 Plaça Bisbe Oliba 3 ☎ 938 86 93 60 🕓 Apr–Sep Tue–Sat 10–7, Sun 10–2; Oct–Mar Tue–Fri 10–1, 3–6, Sat 10–7, Sun 10–2 🖐 Moderate

Plaça Major

Vic's main square is one of the most perfect in Catalonia, where buildings of different styles and ages come together, linked by the uneven arches around their base, to create a satisfying whole. This has always been, above all else, a market place; but to experience its symmetry and beauty, come back when it is empty. Within the square are the Gothic town hall, begun in 1388, and buildings from the Renaissance, baroque and Modernist periods.

🍴 Cafés and bars around the edge (€)

a walk around Vic

The city authorities have created a ruta turística around the old town of Vic. By following this simple walk you get to see all the city's main monuments in a short space of time.

Start at the railway station (the bus station is 100m/110yds from here). Walk down Carrer de Jacint Verdaguer, directly opposite the station entrance, leading to Plaça Major.

The tourist office is close to the town hall, directly ahead of you on the far side of the square. If it is open, pick up the leaflet about the town trail, with descriptions of the various buildings along the way. If not, simply follow the signs marked *Ruta Turística*.

Follow the route by heading down Carrer de la Ciutat behind the town hall, then turning right on to Carrer Miquel de Sants.

Continue on this route as it passes historic houses and baroque churches, as well as a Romanesque bridge, a section of the old city walls and a 2nd-century Roman temple. Eventually you return to Plaça Major, where you can stop for a coffee before returning to the station by a different route.

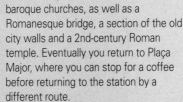

Go down Carrer dels Argenters, the narrow lane in one corner of the square with Forn Sant Miquel on the corner. Reaching a small square, turn left into Carrer de les Escales and go down the steps to reach Rambla del Passeig. Turn left and follow the Ramblas along the course of the old city walls. Turn right when you reach Carrer de Jacint Verdaguer to return to the station.

Distance 3km (2 miles)
Time 1.5 hours
Start/end point Vic station 🚇 13J
🚌 From Girona to nearby bus station
Lunch La Taula (➤ 184)

HOTELS

CALONGE
Park Hotel San Jorge (€€€)
Four-star hotel overlooking a rugged stretch of coastline, with access on foot to a pair of secluded coves.

✉ Carretera de Palamós ☎ 972 65 23 11; www.silken-parksanjorge.com
🕐 All year

LLORET DE MAR
Excelsior (€€)
This seaside hotel features a spa, an excellent restaurant and a terrace on the palm-lined promenade. Most of the 45 rooms have sea views.

✉ Passeig Jacint Verdaguer 16 ☎ 972 36 41 37;
www.excelsiorhotellloret.com 🕐 All year

Gran Hotel Monterrey (€€)
Luxury hotel on the outskirts of the resort, with a swimming pool and tennis courts in extensive grounds.

✉ Carretera Blanes-Tossa de Mar ☎ 972 34 60 54: www.ghmonterrey.com
🕐 All year

Santa Marta (€€€)
Smart, modern hotel set in a pine wood behind the quiet cove of Santa Cristina, with acres of flower gardens and stunning sea views.

✉ Platja Santa Cristina ☎ 972 36 49 04; www.hotelsantamarta.com
🕐 Feb–Nov

PALAMÓS
La Fosca (€)
Modest but comfortable two-star *pension*, set back from the beach in its own quiet bay.

✉ Passeig de la Fosca 24 ☎ 972 60 10 71 🕐 All year

Trias (€€)
Luxury and elegance go hand in hand in this modern beach hotel,

which has a range of facilities including a swimming pool and solarium.

✉ Passeig del Mar ☎ 972 60 18 00; www.hoteltrias.com 🕔 All year

PLATJA D'ARO
Platja Park (€€)
Busy, four-star hotel in the centre of town, with a children's pool and play area and a programme of nightly entertainment. The beach is about 10 minutes' walk away.

✉ Avinguda de Strasburg 10 ☎ 972 81 68 05 🕔 Apr–Oct

Xaloc (€€)
A comfortable, three-star hotel, with a quiet terrace garden leading to the small beach of Platja Rovira.

✉ Cala Rovira ☎ 972 81 73 00 🕔 May–Sep

S'AGARÓ
Hostal de la Gavina (€€€)
The most famous hotel on the Costa Brava was opened in 1924 and designed by the Catalán Modernist architect Rafael Masó in the style of a Gothic villa. Film stars such as Orson Welles and Elizabeth Taylor have stayed here, enjoying its antiques, tapestries and marble floors, its fine Catalán cuisine and its landscaped gardens on a rocky promontory above the sea.

✉ Plaça de la Rosaleda ☎ 972 32 11 00; www.lagavina.com 🕔 Apr–Oct

S'Agaró (€€)
Less exclusive than its famous neighbour, this luxury four-star hotel also has its own extensive gardens, just a short walk from the beach.

✉ Platja Sant Pol ☎ 972 32 52 00; www.hotelsagaro.com 🕔 All year

S'Agaró Mar (€€)
A lovely family hotel with pool, playground and terrace gardens in the pine woods above Sant Pol beach.

✉ Camí de la Caleta ☎ 972 32 11 40 🕔 Apr–Oct

SANT FELIU DE GUÍXOLS
Edén Roc (€€)
Large hotel set in its own grounds beside the cove of Port Salvi. Facilities include a swimming pool and a children's playground.

✉ Port Salvi ☎ 972 32 01 00; www.edenrochotel.com ⏰ Feb–Dec

Plaça (€€)
Comfortable three-star hotel with balconies overlooking the market square, a short way back from the beach.

✉ Plaça Mercat 22 ☎ 972 32 51 55; www.hotelplaza.org ⏰ All year

TOSSA DE MAR
Diana (€€)
Attractive seafront villa, built in the Modernist style with arched windows, stained glass and featuring a fireplace by Antoni Gaudí in the lounge.

✉ Plaça d'Espanya 6 ☎ 972 34 18 86; www.diana-hotel.com ⏰ Apr–Oct

Gran Hotel Reymar (€€€)
Arguably the smartest hotel in Tossa, with a heated swimming pool and tennis courts and a pleasant garden with lovely views looking down over the Mar Menuda beach.

✉ Platja Mar Menuda ☎ 972 34 03 12; www.ghreymar.com ⏰ May–Oct

Mar Menuda (€€)
Peaceful, traditional hotel on the beach of the same name, just around the bay from Tossa's main beach promenade.

✉ Platja Mar Menuda ☎ 972 34 10 00; www.hotelmarmenuda.com
⏰ Jan–Oct

VIC
Ciutat de Vic (€€)
The best choice in town – a smart, modern business hotel on the edge of the historic centre.

✉ Passatge Can Mastrot ☎ 938 89 25 51; www.nh-hotels.com ⏰ All year

Parador de Vic (€€)

This state-run inn was designed in Catalán farmhouse style, and set in a pine grove overlooking a reservoir at the foot of the Montseny mountains. The restaurant serves up hearty Catalán stews and fresh angler fish with garlic mayonnaise. There are wonderful views of the mountains from the outdoor swimming pool.

✉ Pantà de Sau, Carrer de Roda de Ter (14km from Vic) ☎ 938 12 23 23; www.parador.es 🕐 All year

RESTAURANTS

BLANES

Buggy (€€)

On the promenade at the northerrn end of the beach, Buggy specializes in fresh fish and seafood.

✉ Passeig Pau Casals 49 ☎ 972 33 60 64 🕐 Lunch and dinner, Thu–Tue

El Port (€€)

Come here to eat freshly caught fish beneath the harbour walls. The lobster and sea bass are expensive but there is a very affordable set lunch, which features paella, mussels and fresh fish.

✉ Esplanada del Port ☎ 972 33 48 19 🕐 Lunch and dinner daily

El Ventall (€€€)

One of the top restaurants in the area iin a country house between Blanes and Lloret de Mar. The cooking is Mediterranean and modern Catalán.

✉ Carretera de Lloret km2 ☎ 972 33 29 81 🕐 Lunch and dinner Wed–Mon

LLORET DE MAR

Les Petxines (€€€)

New-wave chef Paula Casanovas turns out inventive Catalán-Mediterranean cooking in a surprising venue on the beachfront at Lloret de Mar. If you don't want to splash out, have a salad on the summer terrace.

✉ Passeig Jacint Verdaguer 16 ☎ 972 36 41 37 🕐 Lunch and dinner daily

El Trull (€€€)

Popular fish restaurant overlooking a pretty cove with a terrace with a pool in summer.

✉ Cala Canyelles ☎ 972 36 49 28 🕐 Lunch and dinner daily

PALAMÓS

La Gamba (€€€)

The best local seafood, simply prepared, on a terrace overlooking the harbour. Specialities are prawns, *suquet* casserole (► 14), oven-baked fish and stuffed sea urchins.

✉ Plaça Sant Pere 1 ☎ 972 31 46 33 🕐 Lunch and dinner, Thu–Tue

Maria de Cadaqués (€€€)

Trendy fish restaurant which displays paintings by local artists on the walls. Fish comes fresh from the local fleet.

✉ Carrer Tauler i Servià 6 ☎ 972 31 40 09 🕐 Lunch Tue–Sun, dinner Tue–Sat

PLATJA D'ARO

El Cau del Pernil (€€)

This traditional cellar-bar specializes in ham, as well as several varieties of sausages and charcoal-grilled meat. A meat eater's heaven.

✉ Avinguda Sant Feliu 7 ☎ 972 81 72 09 🕐 Lunch and dinner daily

Fanals Platja (€€–€€€)

Seafood restaurant looking out on to the beach. The specialities, including lobster paella, are expensive, but there are more modestly priced delights on the menu.

✉ Passeig Marítim 92 ☎ 972 81 98 26 🕐 Lunch and dinner daily Apr–Oct, lunch only in winter

SANT FELIU DE GUÍXOLS

Bahía (€€)

Popular fish restaurant on the promenade. Start with a *pica-pica*, a selection of a dozen fishy *tapas*.

✉ Passeig del Mar 17 ☎ 972 32 02 19 🕐 Lunch and dinner daily

Can Salvi (€€)

The emphasis here is on locally caught fish, including anchovies, salmon and sole in Roquefort sauce.

✉ Passeig del Mar 23 ☎ 972 32 10 13 🕐 Lunch and dinner; closed Thu

El Dorado Mar (€€)

Fresh seafood on a terrace overlooking the sea.

✉ Passeig Marítím President Irla 15 ☎ 972 32 62 86 🕐 Lunch and dinner, daily

TOSSA DE MAR
La Cuina de Can Simón (€€€)

Michelin-star restaurant in an old cottage near the town walls offering creative modern Catalán cuisine and a gastronomic menu.

✉ Carrer Portal 24 ☎ 972 34 12 69 🕐 Lunch wed–Sun, sinner Wed–Sat. Open daily in summer

Minerva (€€)

One of a row of seafood restaurants facing the beach at the north end of the bay.

✉ Avinguda Sant Ramón de Penyafort ☎ 972 34 09 39 🕐 Lunch and dinner, daily

Santa Marta (€€)

Pretty terrace restaurant in the heart of the Vila Vella, specializing in fish dishes including *cim-i-tomba*, a monkfish, potato and garlic casserole.

✉ Carrer Francesc Aromir 2 ☎ 972 340472 🕐 Easter–Sep, lunch and dinner Thu–Tue

VIC
Ágape (€)

Hip bookshop-café offering vegetarian and fish dishes and world cuisines. Near the Roman temple.

✉ Carrer Progrés 2 ☎ 938 89 26 46 🕐 Mon–Sat 9–6

Basset (€€)

Arty restaurant featuring modern variations on traditional Catalán cuisine.

✉ Carrer Sant Sadurní 4 ☎ 938 890212 🕔 Lunch and dinner, Mon–Sat

Café Nou (€)

Noisy, bustling locals' pub, packed out on market days. The set menu here is one of the best deals anywhere.

✉ Plaça Major 23 ☎ 938 86 25 02 🕔 Lunch and dinner, Tue–Sun

El Jardinet (€€)

Catalán cooking with a hint of French in a delightful restaurant in the back streets of the old town.

✉ Carrer dels Corretgers 8 ☎ 938 86 28 77 🕔 Lunch Tue–Sun, dinner Tue–Sat

La Taula (€€)

Old mansion in the medieval centre with good choice of *tapas* and main meals. Salt cod dishes are a particular speciality.

✉ Plaça Don Miquel de Clariana 4 ☎ 938 86 32 29 🕔 Lunch Tue–Sun, dinner Tue–Sat

SHOPPING

FOOD AND DRINK

Ca'n Vilada

Carrer dels Argenters has several delicatessens selling the local sausages for which Vic is famous. This shop at the entrance to the lane is one of the best, with pâtés, salads and numerous varieties of sausage.

✉ Placa Major 34, Vic ☎ 938 86 32 59

MARKETS

Blanes – Mon; Caldes de Malavella – Tue; Calonge – Thu; Lloret de Mar – Tue; Palamós – Tue; Platja d'Aro – Fri; Sant Feliu de Guíxols – Sun; Tossa de Mar – Thu; Vic – Tue, Sat

ENTERTAINMENT

BAR
Cala Banys

A ten-minute walk on the cliff path leads to this fashionable cocktail bar overlooking a rocky cove.

✉ Cala Banys, Lloret de Mar ☎ 972 36 55 15 🕐 May–Sep daily 10am–3am; Mar–Apr, Oct Mon–Fri 10–9, Sat–Sun 10am–3am

CASINO
Casino de Lloret

Modern casino with gaming machines, blackjack, roulette and Spanish card games; dinner-dance and cabaret each Saturday evening. A new Gran Casino de Costa Brava is scheduled to open in Lloret in 2008.

✉ Carretr dels Esports 1, Lloret de Mar ☎ 972 36 61 16 🕐 Sun–Thu 7pm–3am, Fri–Sat 7pm–4am

DISCOS

The mega-resorts of Lloret de Mar and Platja d'Aro are the nightlife hotspots of the Costa Brava. During the summer, PR people from the top discos tour the streets handing out free tickets to anyone deemed sufficiently young, sexy and hip. Disco fashions change with the seasons, but long-time favourites include Joy at Platja d'Aro and Tropics at Lloret de Mar. Most discos get busy around midnight and close around 5am.

MUSIC FESTIVALS
Calonge

Concerts are held in the medieval castle each August.

☎ 972 66 17 14

Sant Feliu de Guíxols

One of the top festivals on the Costa Brava, with international musicians appearing at concerts in the parish church in July and August.

☎ 972 82 00 51

Index

Acknowledgements

The Automobile Association would like to thank the following photographers and companies for their assistance in the preparation of this book.

Abbreviations for the picture credits are as follows – (t) top; (b) bottom; (c) centre; (l) left; (r) right; (AA) AA World Travel Library

4l Restaurant, Platja d'Aro, AA/M Chaplow; **4c** Children playing, AA/M Chaplow; **4r** Teatro Museo Dali, Figueres, AA/S Watkins; **5l** Golf, Costa Blanca, AA/M Chaplow; **5c** River Onar through Girona, AA/P Enticknap; **6/7** Restaurant, Platja d'Aro, AA/M Chaplow; **8/9** Pottery for sale, Nijar, AA/M Chaplow; **10/11** Beach at Palamos, AA/M Chaplow; **10c** Medieval House, Pals, AA/P Enticknap; **10bl** Cadaques fisherman, AA/M Chaplow; **10br** Casa-Museo Dali, Portlligat, AA/M Chaplow; **11c** Sant Joan de les Abadesses, AA/M Chaplow; **11b** Costa Brava Beach, AA/M Chaplow; **12/13t** Fish with Romesco sauce, AA/M Chaplow; **12/13b** Restaurant, Plaja d'Aro, AA/M Chaplow; **13t** Pan com tomate, Catalan food, AA/M Chaplow; **13c** Catalan salad, AA/M Chaplow; **13b** Olives, market, Ripoli, AA/P Enticknap; **14t** Tapas Bar, Costa Brava, AA/M Chaplow; **14b** Vin de l'Emporda, AA/M Chaplow; **14/15** Café, near Banyoles, AA/M Chaplow; **15** Crema Catalana, AA/M Chaplow; **16** Diving lesson, AA/C Sawyer; **16/17** Fish market, AA/M Jourdan; **17c** Traditional Catalan meal, AA/J A Tims; **17b** Girona, AA/P Enticknap; **18/19t** Castell Gala Dali, Pubol, AA/M Chaplow; **18/19b** Ceramic pottery, AA/M Chaplow; **19t** El Port de la Selva, AA/M Chaplow; **19c** Beach at San Sebastian, AA/M Jourdan; **20/21** Children playing, AA/M Chaplow; **24** Festival Havaneras, AA/M Chaplow; **27** Costa Blanca Express, AA/M Chaplow; **28/29** Bus, Costa Blanca, AA/K Paterson; **32** Policeman, AA/M Jourdan; **34/35** Teatro Museo Dali, Figueres, AA/S Watkins; **36t** Cadaques Bay, AA/S Watkins; **36b** Fishing Boats, Cadaques Beach, AA/S Watkins; **37** Bridge over River Fluvia, Besalu, AA/P Enticknap; **38** Cadaques, AA/M Chaplow; **40** Castell Gala Dali, Pubol, AA/M Chaplow; **40/41** Crypt at Castell Gala Dali, AA/M Chaplow; **41** Dali's Cadillac, Castell Gala Dali, AA/M Chaplow; **42** El Rentador, Castello d'Empuries, AA/M Chaplow; **42/43** Castello d'Empuries, AA/M Chaplow; **44** Girona, AA/P Enticknap; **44/45** Houses, Girona, AA/M Chaplow; **45** Banys Arabs, Girona, AA/M Chaplow; **46** Beach, Bahia de Roses, AA/S Watkins; **46/47** Sant Pere de Rodes, AA/M Chaplow; **47** Sant Pere de Rodes, AA/M Chaplow; **48/49t** Photographing bird, AA/S Watkins; **48/49b** Parc Natural de l'Aiguamolls de l'Emporda, AA/M Chaplow; **50** Citadel, Roses, AA/S Watkins; **50/51** Roses, AA/M Chaplow; **52/53** Teatre-Museu Dali in Figueres, AA/M Chaplow; **54/55** Tossa de Mar, AA/M Chaplow; **56/57** Golf, Costa Blanca, AA/M Chaplow; **58/59** Tapas Bar, AA/M Jourdan; **59** Card players in Tapas Bar, AA/C Sawyer; **60/61** Fisherman, AA/M Jourdan; **62** Casa de Sola Morales, AA/M Chaplow; **63** Placa Major, Banyoles, AA/M Chaplow; **65** Ceramics for sale, La Bisbal, AA/M Chaplow; **66/67** Beach, Blanes, AA/M Chaplow; **68** Children playing, AA/M Chaplow; **70/71** Cap de Creus, AA/M Chaplow; **72/73** Golf course, AA/J Poulsen; **74/75** Medieval town of Besalu, AA/M Chaplow; **76/77** Beach, Palamos, AA/M Chaplow; **78/79** City of Girona, AA/P Enticknap; **81** Volca de Montascopa, near Olot, AA/M Chaplow; **83** Banys Arabs, Girona, AA/M Chaplow; **84** Call Jueu, Girona, AA/M Chaplow; **85** Placa dels Apostols, Girona, AA/M Chaplow; **86/87** Girona, AA/P Enticknap; **88/89** View along river in Girona, AA/M Chaplow; **90/91** Museo d'Art, Girona, AA/M Chaplow; **91** Museo d'Art, Girona, AA/M Chaplow; **92** Restaurant, Girona, AA/M Chaplow; **93** Aiguablava, AA/P Enticknap; **95** Pottery, La Bisbal, AA/M Chaplow; **96/97** Calella de Palafrugell, AA/M Chaplow; **96** Market, Palafrugell, AA/P Enticknap; **98/99** Castellfolit de la Roca, AA/M Chaplow; **100** Medes Island, AA/M Chaplow; **100/101** Glass bottomed boat tour, AA/M Chaplow; **102/103** Olot, AA/M Chaplow; **103** Olot, AA/M Chaplow; **104/105** Rambla Casal dels Volcans, Olot, AA/M Chaplow; **106** Olot, AA/M Chaplow; **107** Garrotxa Natural Park, Olot, AA/M Chaplow; **109** Pals, AA/M Chaplow; **110** Shopping, AA/K Paterson; **111** Sant Joan de las Abadesses, AA/M Chaplow; **112** Tamariu AA/M Chaplow; **113** Torroella de Montgri, AA/M Chaplow; **114/115** Tamariu beach, AA/M Chaplow; **116** Ullastret, AA/M Chaplow; **129** Serra de l'Albera, AA/M Chaplow; **130/131** Cine-Teatre Jardi, Figueres, AA/M Chaplow; **131** Castell de Sant Ferran, Figueres, AA/M Chaplow; **132/133** Narcis Monturoil, Figueres, AA/M Chaplow; **134** Dali Museum, Figueres, AA/P Enticknap; **137** Cap de Creus, AA/M Chaplow; **138** Castello d'Empuries, AA/M Chaplow; **138/139** Castello d'Empuries, AA/M Chaplow; **140/141** La Escala, AA/P Enticknap; **142** Port de la Selva, AA/M Chaplow; **143** Port Lligat, AA/S Watkins; **144/145** Rosas, AA/M Chaplow; **146** Sant Pere Pescador, AA/M Chaplow; **147** Sant Pere Pescador, beach, AA/M Chaplow; **148/149** Serra de l'Albera, AA/M Chaplow; **157** Montseny, AA/M Chaplow; **158** Blanes, AA/M Chaplow; **159** Windsurfers, AA/A Koupranioff; **160/161** Caldes de Malavella, AA/M Chaplow; **162** Lloret de Mar, AA/M Chaplow; **162/163** Sant Roma in Lloret de Mar, AA/M Chaplow; **164/165** Porta Ferrada, AA/M Chaplow; **166/167** Santa Maria church, Palamos, AA/M Chaplow; **167** Platja d'Aro, AA/M Chaplow; **167** Platja d'Aro, AA/M Chaplow; **168** Coastline, Costa Blanca, AA/M Chaplow; **169** Casino la Constancia in Sant Feliu de Guixols, AA/M Chaplow; **170** Montseny National Park, AA/P Enticknap; **170/171** Serra de Montseny, AA/M Chaplow; **172** Placa Major, Vic, AA/M Chaplow; **173** Cathedral, Vic, AA/M Chaplow; **174/175** Placa Major, Vic, AA/M Chaplow; **175** Placa Major, Vic, AA/M Chaplow; **176/177** Placa Major, Vic, AA/M Chaplow

Every effort has been made to trace the copyright holders, and we apologise in advance for any accidental errors. We would be happy to apply the corrections in the following edition of this publication.

Sight locator index

This index relates to the maps on the covers. We have given map references to the main sights in the book. Grid references in italics indicate sights featured on the town plan. Some sights within towns may not be plotted on the maps.

Dear Reader

Your comments, opinions and recommendations are very important to us. Please help us to improve our travel guides by taking a few minutes to complete this simple questionnaire.

You do not need a stamp (unless posted outside the UK). If you do not want to cut this page from your guide, then photocopy it or write your answers on a plain sheet of paper.

Send to: **The Editor, AA World Travel Guides, FREEPOST SCE 4598, Basingstoke RG21 4GY.**

Your recommendations...
We always encourage readers' recommendations for restaurants, nightlife or shopping – if your recommendation is used in the next edition of the guide, we will send you a **FREE AA Guide** of your choice from this series. Please state below the establishment name, location and your reasons for recommending it.

_____
_____
_____
_____
_____
_____

Please send me **AA Guide** _____

About this guide...
Which title did you buy?
 AA _____
Where did you buy it? _____
When? m m / y y
Why did you choose this guide? _____
_____
_____
_____
_____

Did this guide meet your expectations?

Exceeded ☐ Met all ☐ Met most ☐ Fell below ☐

Were there any aspects of this guide that you particularly liked? _____
_____
_____
_____

continued on next page...

Is there anything we could have done better? _____

_____

_____

_____

About you...
Name (*Mr/Mrs/Ms*) _____

Address _____

_____

_____ Postcode _____

Daytime tel nos _____

Email _____

Please only give us your mobile phone number or email if you wish to hear from us about other products and services from the AA and partners by text or mms, or email.

Which age group are you in?
Under 25 ☐   25–34 ☐   35–44 ☐   45–54 ☐   55–64 ☐   65+ ☐

How many trips do you make a year?
Less than one ☐   One ☐   Two ☐   Three or more ☐

Are you an AA member? Yes ☐   No ☐

About your trip...
When did you book? m m / y y   When did you travel? m m / y y

How long did you stay? _____

Was it for business or leisure? _____

Did you buy any other travel guides for your trip? _____

If yes, which ones? _____

_____

_____

Thank you for taking the time to complete this questionnaire. Please send it to us as soon as possible, and remember, you do not need a stamp (*unless posted outside the UK*).

AA Travel Insurance call 0800 072 4168 or visit www.theAA.com